RITUALS FOR CLIMATE CHANGE

Before you start to read this book, take this moment to think about making a donation to punctum books, an independent non-profit press

@ https://punctumbooks.com/support

If you're reading the e-book, you can click on the image below to go directly to our donations site. Any amount, no matter the size, is appreciated and will help us to keep our ship of fools afloat. Contributions from dedicated readers will also help us to keep our commons open and to cultivate new work that can't find a welcoming port elsewhere. Our adventure is not possible without your support.

Vive la Open Access.

Fig. 1. Detail from Hieronymus Bosch, *Ship of Fools*
(1490–1500)

First published in 2023 by 3Ecologies Books/Immediations,
an imprint of punctum books.
https://punctumbooks.com

ISBN-13: 978-1-68571-112-2 (print)
ISBN-13: 978-1-68571-113-9 (ePDF)

DOI: 10.53288/0451.1.00

LCCN: 2023942106
Library of Congress Cataloging Data is available from the Library of Congress

Book design: Vincent W.J. van Gerven Oei
Cover image: Naomi Ortiz, *Mending*. ©2020.

Rituals for Climate Change: A Crip Struggle for Ecojustice is supported in part by the National Association of Latino Arts and Cultures and the Ford Foundation through funding from the Reclaiming the US/Mexico Border Narrative Grant Program.
https://www.nalac.org/grants/nalac-fund-for-the-arts/border-narrative-change-grant/.

Connect with Naomi further at:
https://www.NaomiOrtiz.com/

spontaneous acts of scholarly combustion

HIC SVNT MONSTRA

Naomi Ortiz

Rituals for Climate Change
A Crip Struggle for Ecojustice

Contents

To all who care for land, water, seeds,
air, plants, ancestors, people, and all
the creatures of the places we live.
Remember, we are many.

THE CALL

Fig. 1. "Canción" © 2022 Naomi Ortiz. Sandstone cliff walls and formation. A raven flies and their larger shadow glides over the cliff. A flowing plant grows in a patch of dirt on the side of a cliff.

Canción de las Hermanas

We are beautiful formations
in the last wild stretch of blue horizon
and juniper

The shadows
who live on our canyon walls
trace slick contours
the solid outline of our borders

We here, sisters eternal
Red swirl sandstone
Endure change that splinters the sides
of our bodies
We shed what is ready to be released

From pockets hidden in our layers
sweet tones and base boom echoes
stories sung beneath the surface

Once a river ran between our legs
poured through sage-studded thighs
followed the pull
to wander past
your human
inattentive gaze

                    outran our will
                and sank to where words
                    find no light

            And once our ribs were sought for sanctuary
                        to cradle tender flesh
                        in deep dark of night
                    to find rest in our bosom
                    steadied in the long hours
                            before dawn

    And once wind swept hair out of our eyes
    our ancient faces like honeycomb
    gazes deserving of pilgrimage
    Lizards mated, in the length of our shade
    Dried and blessed umbilical cords
    sprinkled dust
    caught on our lashes

                        Our memory houses rhythms
                        beat in unison to our wonder
                        eons have salted our skin
                        dried us to be devoured
                        by shuffle, scamper of claw
                        Only *nuestras primas,* the stars
                        have outlived our time

    Tell us you desire to taste our abandon
    brace against our wisdom
    it is what we still have to give
    as we weather your distracted race
    toward extinction

THE LISTENING

Fig. 2. "Home" © 2015 Naomi Ortiz. Contracted hand and forearm are in the middle of the painting, palm side up. One half of the painting is a daytime desert scene showing cacti and mountains. The sun is the shape of a human heart. Roots go from the soil into the arm. The other half of the painting is a nighttime desert scene. Cacti and mountains are shown in moonlight. The moon is the shape of a human heart. A moonbeam goes from the moon into the arm.

Invitation

Rain pounds into earth
Sand expands as it soaks, absorbs, gets soft
    This is the moment
        when life has a chance

Water surges down riverbeds which minutes ago lay
    barren and dry
Seeds battered by rocky soil, sense spaciousness below
seize the moment to send out roots, spring forth shoots

The dark stillness of underground
becomes full of surprises as
scorpions and centipedes drawn by rain
trek from hidden burrows beneath the surface
through downpour and wind, chaos and change
find their way to each other to dance and mate

    The desert knows the best times to undress desire

This rolling monsoon storm draws us out to the porch
I like to go to the edge, to be within kissing distance of
    danger
You prefer the cozy confidence of shelter, staying close
    to the door

Chaos of storm
rattles windowpanes
awakens senses
Scent of creosote soaks into tongue
throat and lungs
Makes me want to   just
                      breathe
                            deeper

Watching rain buck and twist, till it slaps to the ground
this release of building tension, loosens our shoulders
wakes us both from the drowsiness of heat, the labor of
     being
       Startles us into now

A sudden drop in temperature, wind runs cool through
     my hair
Makes me remember how much my fingertips love to
     feel you
I caress the crease of an elbow, the sun-stained skin
     etched on the back of your neck
Urgency crackles wet, crashes into my body
unsheathes a bit of joy I had tucked inside

Somehow today, we find each other
in the middle of this chaos and change
Possess this moment
to cherish soft tenderness as flesh greets moisture

       This desert knows the best times to undress desire

Future Orientation

My partner and I always start
this conversation at a terrible time
of right before bed or
in the middle of paying bills

I ask, "If the city runs out of water, do you think...
we will lose our home?
You know,
have anywhere to go?"

My partner   slows   to   stop

As two Crips, our worry conversations once focused
on how to stay out of institutional settings
as we grew old, or
work and family drama
Now
they are shallow breath, full-throat effort
to imagine how to best be prepared

My partner replies,
calm tone for us both,
"We are in a lot better spot living in the city versus
    unmanaged rural areas.
It will take a while for the groundwater to run out.

But yeah, if that happens, we may just need to leave and
    lose everything."

I look into their face which mirrors mine
rigid pose to mask fear

I know this answer is coming, but
every time I ask, I hope that
somehow, this time, there will be
some new piece of information or a detail overlooked
in the shadows beyond the pools of lamplight
that one of us will spontaneously recognize
to plot our way through
what was once thought extraordinary
turned real

The Hunt

In the desert, we peck for moisture everywhere
labor to crack open mesquite's fibrous pods
before sticky seeds turn to stone

A race against dry, only a matter of time
    precipitation must sink or rise
pull away from itself
    alchemize air
        or trust gravity
            saturate slowly
                through stones, sand, compact dirt
                        to gather

Precious water
  she cannot help but embrace   everything she touches
                PFOS...GenX...PFAS[1] from

1   "Per- and polyfluoroalkyl substances (PFAS) are a group of man-made chemicals that includes PFOA, PFOS, GenX, and many other chemicals. PFAS have been manufactured and used in a variety of industries around the globe, including in the United States since the 1940s. Both chemicals are very persistent in the environment and in the human body – meaning they don't break down and they can accumulate over time. There is evidence that exposure to PFAS can lead to adverse human health effects." "PFAS Explained," *Environmental Protection Agency*, April 10, 2023, https://www.epa.gov/pfas/pfas-explained.

training to manage catastrophe's rage
non-stick technology tricks
poisons permeate

all trickle down

Caliche thick protector
but aquifer has no boundaries

Open　　　Trusting　　　Vulnerable

It is easier to talk about plumes in the wellfield,
　　groundwater migration
than witness　an　embrace　so　fully　accepting

It is hard to not recoil from that kind of love
　　　　　　　　even as we ask her for more　　and more
　　　　　　　　　　and more

To Stick My Head in the Sand

"How dare you!" – Greta Thunberg[1]

I want to watch three television seasons straight
through from Friday night to Sunday – to drown the
nagging thoughts out

Get in my truck and drive out to a vista, just to see what
I cannot bear to lose, meshed together, instead of each
individual cactus and desert tree with its own story

Push my head deeper into the pillow, close my eyes
when parched wind blusters outside the window

Stop staring up at the sky where monsoon clouds should
be – (my younger self would never have believed they
did not come)

Every rhythm disrupted – except man-made ones:
                                        alarm clock rings morning

1   NDTV, "'How Dare You?': 16-Year-Old Greta Thunberg Thunders At
      UN Climate Summit," *YouTube*, September 24, 2019, https://www.
      youtube.com/watch?v=M1o3NCPKZ4U.

AC clicks on at preset temperature
radio hour smart-ass
work arrival by 9am deadline

I cling to what I control

Ode to Plastic Cups

"The goal is for *no trash* to be sent to landfills,
incinerators or the ocean."[1]

Weight of both reusable glass plus liquid means
my wrist twists down
the only direction it bends
sends drink to splash on carpets or slippery floor

Worse yet
non-flexing elbow means arm
smacks cup across room with accidental gusto
                                at least once a week
Beloved coffee cups
shatter into h u n d r e d s of p i e c e s
must dredge energy to clean up now
hot beverages, my expensive habit

At restaurants, I have to ask for a straw
slick perspiring drink
pointless to even try to lift

1   *Wikipedia,* s.v. "Zero waste," https://en.wikipedia.org/wiki/Zero_
waste.

to lips with fingers, hand, shoulder
Instead, I bat and slide glass across tabletop
position straw below mouth, sip
then push it back, nudge, shift

Except, every once in a while, I miscalculate
or glass bottom catches on table surface
to topple and douse eating companion with cold
    beverage
saturate my clothes and shoes good

Unless the cup is plastic

Oh, chemically bonded vessel, with your springy
    forgiveness
to bounce passively on floor, patiently listless
you wait for me to retrieve you in my own time

Oh, plastic cup
with your bright shiny colors
your fun designs
your resilient sides
As scooter squeezes you between wheel and wall
you may bend, but do not crack where you lie

Weight light, large brim
I can sip straight from the rim

Glossy red party cups sold in long plastic bags
last me month-long jags
I stock up, dollar store deals
just what works for my body
call it an accommodation
this need for plastic cups

As disabled person
independence is precarious

daily life and reason
constructed upon a wobbly set of Crip hacks
get me from, *can't* to *good enough*

Where is my place in zero waste?

Suppression

Spruce-fir forest of the Pinaleño Mountains
    home for subspecies of squirrel
brown fur, light-colored paws
    found only here in all the world

Mount Graham Red Squirrel
    They know the precious nature of seeds, mushrooms,
    insects, eggs
           Future   Food
    Food   Future

Territory – they try to protect
    defend the spot they claim

Chatter calls upon sight of intruder
    squeaks and barks given in long series
growls at potential threats increase intensity if the
    danger does not diminish
They give fair warning before propelling tiny body to
    fight

Loyal tree home devotion creates
    faithful stewards to only today
then – to tomorrow

109 endangered squirrels[1] have daytime to fight for life
      to scavenge food, build middens
Their demise belongs to the night

Three observatories sit, big white domes cracked open to
      ponder starlit sky
        Back burns to remove trees
suppression a.k.a. control = observatories are safe

These little squirrels who explore with their black
      nimble whiskers
analyze through tan-rimmed eyes
      are territorial they say
Do not reproduce enough to keep up
      with destruction of habitat
blame instincts honed over hundreds of generations

Too fierce is reason to pivot fault
      – leave unprotected

---

1   Claire Chandler, "Arizona's Mount Graham Red Squirrel Makes
Comeback, But Not Out of the Woods Yet," *Tucson.com,* November
17, 2020, https://tucson.com/news/local/arizonas-mount-graham-
red-squirrel-makes-comeback-but-not-out-of-the-woods-yet/
article_f4fda664-723b-58db-bfa7-7b483a82636c.html.

Interlude 1

Holding my wheelrims securely, I look down the steep slope of ponderosa pine and shrubs watching as their shadows stretch and lengthen. A voice calls me over. My partner and an assortment of strangers assemble into a loose group. The guide looks around, his gaze pauses and then lingers on me before taking in the other people gathered, and asks, "What brought you up the mountain to spend a few hours looking at stars?" When my partner and I say we are celebrating our first anniversary, the guide laughs incredulously, responding, "Really!?" Surprised, I stare at him in disbelief. Maybe $50 a ticket is nothing to him, but when we came across a two-for-one coupon to stargaze through one of the largest telescopes open to the public, we snatched the chance to go and celebrate our anniversary with an adventure. The guide, still amused, turns and leads the group past old forest service buildings repurposed for the needs of the observatory, which sits perched on the pine-topped mountain cascading up out of the desert.

The observatory itself is not wheelchair accessible. However, I have been assured that once inside, a lot of the positions of the lens eyepiece can be seen through when seated. I swallow down the frustration of this irony as my partner, the guide, and I disassemble my manual chair to carry it up the 5 stairs to the viewing platform.

I fight back feeling guilty about making this choice. I know many disabled folks could not deal with this exclusion and ableism by simply taking their chair apart and crawling up the stairs, nor should they be expected to. But sometimes ableism smacks into a lifelong dream that has a coupon. So, my partner and I agreed to compromise our usually strict adherence to not go where other disabled people are barred from going. The guide tells us that there are long-term plans to build out from the observatory and create an ADA[1]-accessible entrance. This does not appease me.

Scooting up the stairs on my butt and onto the floor of the main room, I help reassemble my chair and awkwardly climb back in. Once in my chair, the other stargazers relax out of their discomfort and we get busy looking up into the depths. The temperature drops and I put on all of the sweaters I brought, my jacket, hat, gloves, and scarf. Still shivering, I run my hands over my legs trying to build up the friction of warmth. Like a dance, I move in and out of line to see bright sparkly objects pulsing, ever moving through the night sky.

I cannot remember a time when my breath did not slow, when my body did not relax and melt into the ground as I looked up at the stars. I grew up with a love affair centered around the depths of this mysterious sky. On my street, in whichever neighborhood my family had rented an apartment in that year, the stars held a familiarity of place. The constellations made up a visual soundtrack of late-evening conversations sitting in a friend's car or to the magical moments I caught as a kid to sit outside alone at night. The stars have always been witnesses to my questions and contemplations.

1   Americans with Disabilities Act.

As a kid, the stories I was taught about the constellations were not the stories of my ancestors. Their stories were both burned out of their mouths and numbed away. Constellation names became empty placeholders where I would make up my own meanings and create my own picture shapes from lessons at school or day-to-day neighborhood observations. In my imagination, the North Star became the Harriet Tubman Star. Orion's belt and tiny head (usually stars I could pick out in the city) I imagined as a construction worker, their hammer hanging ready to be used. Mostly, I instinctively trusted that the stars kept their own stories safe.

Near the end of the night, the guide asks us to line up to see Andromeda, the nearest galaxy. Slowly, I roll forward as the line of people shrinks down to me. I am not sure what I expect. I grew up watching the "galaxies" in *Star Trek: The Next Generation* fly by the starship window. For many childhood years, these pinpricks of light on the TV screen were my only reference to what planets and other galaxies looked like.

Peering down through the eyepiece, I make out a large looking pale gray smudge. At that moment the guide was rattling off information. Andromeda is the closest galaxy to ours and twice the size. I feel my stomach drop, as if experiencing a seasickness of spaciousness.

I like to think I can find the same amount of awe in a seed or when gazing down into a rocky canyon. Yet, I am such a human of this time. Unimpressed by the miracles of everyday life, I am only brought to my humble gooey center by being confronted with the realization that I am a small speck swallowed by an ocean of space.

Later that week, I sit outside in a parking lot wrapped up in my favorite hoodie staring up at the night sky with only my own eyes. My heartbeat slows, swells with perspective and humility. These stars have been a constant in my world. Simply shining. Simply by existing. I am inspired by their gift. I find myself wanting to know more.

Goals

We want people to be politicized
but do not know what to give but
data to illustrate the evidence
414 parts per million – concentration of carbon dioxide in our atmosphere[1]
hottest August, second driest monsoon ever recorded[2]
pledged like plastic cling wrap
we hope will seal the truth in
(without leakage)

When is there a good time to confront change?
We joke about realities, play around with facts
hope ignorance covers the putrid smell
of the pile of garbage
rotting next to the front door
in the can with cracked lid
because it is one more thing we have to deal with

1 Rebecca Lindsey, "Climate Change: Atmospheric Carbon Dioxide," *NOAA Climate.gov*, June 23, 2022, https://www.climate.gov/news-features/understanding-climate/climate-change-atmospheric-carbon-dioxide.

2 Jeff Gardner, "How Dry We Are: Monsoon 2020 Second Worst in the Record Books," *Tucson Weekly*, October 1, 2020, https://www.tucsonweekly.com/TheRange/archives/2020/10/01/how-dry-we-are-monsoon-2020-second-worst-in-the-record-books.

in a day of car doesn't start, boss upset, kid with cough
body push through, get home late, make some kind of
dinner

What to do with this information
who knows what to do with it?

Nature Defined

Nature is in the edges between this world and the next
ICU breathing tube, feeding tube
where I hold her arm around oven-mitt-padded hands
to not disturb the steady beat of interventions fueling
    life

At the edge of the parking lot
a plastic bottle rolls off wind's tongue
I get to know nature from the formerly unnoticed
cusp of human dominated and wild

She surprises me outside my door
baby mesquite tree shades ants pillaging our bounty
orange sunset pink clouds, golden peach bloom into
    night

She reminds me how to push on, births dawn
pale light outlines bed
bookshelf holds tattered journals, pictures of mi familia,
    all my earrings
and my love, a sheet-draped hip silhouette
sprawled long length toe dip off the mattress

Nature sits with us at the old wooden table
drinking ginger beer and rum with lime

pricks my skin with splinters of laughter
venting the day to make space for tomorrow

I offer nature tribute
water
fruit
for quail, rabbits, javelinas, ancestors

Nature responds with jokes in the form of sweat
which drips, drips
curls down spine
laces neck with grime
keeps me cool but cranky as I wait to pick my niece up
    from work

Nature puckers in the still air between strangers
clustered behind bus stop shade slats
waiting out baby wail cacophony
with patience somehow found in reserve
Help a young mother carry on the stroller

Nature is in the relationship of one living thing with
    another
she recognizes my scent
nuzzles my chest when I roll out
onto dirt road, scooter propelled
Cacti, creosote, brittlebush, red and gray rocks

She welcomes me with open sky

Epicenter

Body
ground zero
for how we are instructed to control the world

Limitlessness is the goal
Tap mountain spine
dig deeper to pierce vein
Bulldozers crush, pinch, scrape, screech
compress rock into cactus flesh
cover sheltered baby cub burrow
Siphon riches from cattle
shoulder to shoulder in pens
Efficient production ends in abundant effluent

Body is to straddle
home known through sour, sweet, salty
and a reality sold to us as smooth, pale, infinite
Pump cortisol to do it all but
shame curdles the milked effort

To have a body is to whisper
confessions of desire
Skeleton compound mineral rich
organs fluid function
To live is to be bound by what cannot be overcome

learn to follow body's lead

Bodies dream, wake, move, fall
        consent to touch
exert boundaries in
        yes, yass, YES
or, *No, not tonight*

Bodies host life
        bacteria dwells in eyebrows, guts, tongues
Cells regenerate for function
        Choice is chemical reaction dependent
Eyes dilate – foot pushes brake
        for roadrunner
as they streak across the pavement
        lizard tail swings from beak

Mestize body knits together borders
        learns to use thighs, instead of words, to grip on to
    parent hips
Hold tight above the quake of
        their hands busy tracing the void of everything left
    behind
Nursed with tales of loss and liberation as two sides of
    one

Disabled body inhabits a valley having tested the edge
        Where cane, wheel, words tipped off the ledge
To live with holes, rips, stains
        is to let life wait for now
To lay down and rest

Parts Ready for Ritual

Period
proof bloody red
that my body pays attention
to cycles and rhythms
I would much rather ignore

Tongue tastes air
burnt tang puckers dusty dry
or sometimes fresh juicy sweet
Everyday scent always different
as I sit in the same spot

Skin tries to tell me
sun sits in sky
closer   longer
soon summer
comes

Heart whispers silent prayers
to surrender yet continues
to endure this shift
beginning to eclipse comfort

Uterus sheds body bleeds
Womb I carry

is familiar with change
Settles in
to ride out response
to each call
every spasm

Mind judges body traitor
longs for sameness
but vagina occupied with other worries
Cramps pierce the illusion of safety

Mind begs hands to cling
to what can be held
would rather stay still, cup misery
then reach out to greet uncertainty

Yet, body is undeterred by these requests and
    accusations
continues being self, despite wishes otherwise

How can I resist this vessel
which only answers full truth
to ritual demand?

There is no ready or not ready
only happening now

Ovaries recite
muscles remind
        this is a different kind of trusting myself

One Drop or the Whole Heart?

To avoid our tainted wells, drink water pumped uphill in
    concrete cradled canals from
red-silt-laced Colorado River usurped
south of Lake Havasu, moved through Tonopah Desert
to Phoenix, Scottsdale
down through the Superstition Mountains
hundreds of miles
into Sonoran Desert and Tucson

Try
    to use water wisely
Turn water off when washing dishes, brushing teeth
Plant native cacti that can rely on rain given
Take short showers, use low-flo toilets

Write congresspeople when: Millions of gallons of
regional groundwater are drained, dropping the
water table to build a political promise, a pledge to
stop potential migration but an actual end to... 41
environmental and other regulations[1] suspended to blast

---

1   John Burnett, "Border Wall Rising in Arizona, Raises Concerns
among Conservationists, Native Tribes," *NPR*, October 13, 2019,
https://www.npr.org/2019/10/13/769444262/border-wall-rising-in-
arizona-raises-concerns-among-conservationists-native-trib.

mountains, bulldoze jaguar (javelina, lizard, butterfly,
mule deer) habitat, and dry Quitobaquito springs,
the only natural desert spring where the endangered
Sonoyta mud turtle lives (lived?)

Add my voice to many voices of Tohono O'odham
community members, tribal leaders, and allies as they
are gassed defending sacred land

> "I hate that word, protest," she said. "We are not
> activists, we are not protesting, we are O'odham and this
> is O'odham land."
> – Akimel O'odham demonstrator[2]

Rules and regulations to protect wastewater
therefore groundwater
are loosened, unenforced, tossed out the window
so extraction can speed up before the change that is
    crashing down
the one they call *hoax,* moves us aside
to stay

---

2   Alisa Reznick, "Standoff with Border Patrol, National Park Service
    Ends in Scuffle with Indigenous-Led Demonstrators," *Arizona
    Public Media,* September 22, 2020, https://news.azpm.org/p/news-
    splash/2020/9/22/180618-stand-off-with-border-patrol-national-
    park-service-ends-in-scuffle-with-indigenous-led-demonstrators/.

Ceremony Is Unsettling

A strange consequence of this climate change dread, which seeps in through the cracks of my day-to-day, is the neglect of what I love.

It has been over a month since I have been out to the desert. I feel drawn and at the same time repelled.

As a child, I did not understand the immense privilege of living near land that has never been plowed over or stripped away. All I understood was – desert as sanctuary.

There, Refuge

The apartment stinks of anger and disdain
The odor sets, stains carpet, walls
a residue no amount of cleaning removes

Hand, mouth, fork, spun with his disappointment
until, out front door, air moves slowly, free
across blacktop road
I escape into desert untouched

Rocks speak the language of love
anticipate nothing but time
kept company by lichen ready to
revive with rain's caress

Mummified tarantula stands permanently
on ledge of sand below boulder
thick fuzzy legs surround its own eternity
made nest by black beetle with orange wings

Under sun-drenched sky
bobcats, turtles, tarantula hawks, and I
pick out a path over hardpacked dirt
and splaying thorns

Daytime is for survival, is for staying silent
only ants are oblivious to the harsh circumstances
as they skip and hop across heat-soaked ground
I admire this nimble dedication, they are never afraid

When storms roll through
within minutes water plumps moss
ocotillos and palo verdes sprout leaves
whole desert shifts from brown to brilliant green

I touch what is possible, after just one storm
Wish for change to bloom its way in
through the slats in the window blinds
to cast immediate, joyful, vivid transformation

Thorns aflame in setting sun, model crystal clear
        defense of self
Coyote song heralds in the night
one pack sings, then another
it is a respect thing – to know where to watch your back

In the dark, safety is relative
all movement is to consume what is available, what is
        offered
one learns to stay out of the way
to camouflage body on mattress

Refuge sought out in cool breeze
amongst the slithering sounds, rustles, and pops
tuck pantlegs into socks
as to not appear a hiding place for a creature seeking,
        breathing
just like me

Startled by wing kiss
moths brush cheek on way to pollinate night blooms
in moonlight, cholla silhouettes glisten
ears still ring from inside screams

There, stone made seat
cradles my tender longing
I brace against a love language I understand
only visible by the glow of Grandmother Moon

Ceremony Is Medicine

The desert asked for nothing. Gave unquestioning sanctuary.

An intense ecosystem, a co-mingling of strength with surrender, kept me captivated.

Change comes slow to the desert. Forty-year-old saguaros swaddled in gritty dirt are about the height of a fire hydrant. By 95–100 years in age, the cactus can reach a height of 15–16 feet, and is ready to produce its first arm. By two hundred years old, the saguaro has reached its full height, reaching upwards of 45 feet tall.[1] Slow growth gifts age. Most desert plants will easily outlive me.

This deliberate pace modeled a steadiness I did not find within my home or my body. Seen as too young to give consent, I endured the powerlessness of doctors deciding on invasive surgical intrusions. During the years I spent in bed mending, I felt the land waiting for me.

Out my window, I could glimpse a patch of the area I liked to roam. Day in and day out, I watched for transitions which came not so much with the seasons, but with rain. After the last drops had faded, and the

[1] "Saguaro Cactus," *National Park Service*, January 6, 2016, https://www.nps.gov/orpi/learn/nature/saguaro-cactus.htm.

sky had shaken off the dust to reveal its brilliant blue, the plump green flesh of cacti was left highlighted in the clear shimmering light. The moisture reanimated green lichen and moss on the side of rocks leaving the landscape a completely different shade than before the storm.

From afar, the desert offered consistent rhythms, while I grappled with the isolative, roller-coaster shifts of what my body could or could not do.

Self-Discovery

In bed with the boredom of pain
mind wanders into past, present, future
never in line, always skipping around
my history, their complaints, TV storylines swirl
into a mashup of what came before
Mostly I obsess into a future understanding of who I am
what I can be

Close eyes, yellow outlines the ceiling's negative space
over thick white plaster casts, each leg encased
Only interaction, out my window
the clacking of creosote bush limbs under dusty sky
I want to be intentional about time
Instead, I lay here, dig at confusion and worry with this
    spoon
scrape away at the compacted dirt of my truth
Despite the ache, the effort, I gouge against the grain

I wonder at this hardness
did it come from me
or just what was baked in from my ancestral seeds?

I want signs
instead
I get dreams

Disability Explained

1.

Disability is the embodiment of multiple truths at once
It is the description of the ever-changing direction of
    wind
Nimble focus to which way one must scream the loudest

It is both understimulation and overstimulation
Not being touched for years and being touched too often
    without permission

Disability, in other's eyes, overrules all my other
    identities
Welcome to the equal playing field of the fear of
    vulnerability

It is living in everyone's expectation that if they are nice
    about their ableism
then that
for me
should be enough

2.

Slivers of doubt become trusted tools for survival
    Can I do this? Will they be there? Is there space for
  the tides change of my shifting needs?

Be prepared   for   anything Be   prepared   for
                           anything

3.

Unclenching my hypervigilance allows me to unfold my
  blanket of empathy
Many people rest here for a time
There is safety with the one who does not belong
What they do not realize is there is so much power in
  discovering how to not need to belong
A gift to understand that you can never fit in and
an offering to name for others that universal feeling of
  never fitting in

4.

Disability is a forced exploration of every system Man
  has created to help those who cannot function in
  capitalism
    who require medical access, who need help in
  their home, or for whom being in love is deemed
  inappropriate

Systematic excavation –
    We learn secret ways through concealed tunnels
      We learn to be silent and take what we can find

5.

Disability is living multiple levels at once
Awareness, vulnerability, empathy, humor, anger, focus,
    resistance, creativity
It takes planning for me to be here

Disability is embracing *sustainable,* instead of *healthy,* as
    the label of betterment
Asking what will keep one going, in a way that keeps
    giving

6.

I do not count on anyone being comfortable around me
except maybe other Disabled people
and then only sometimes
We have been convinced that Disability is something we
    should peel off
keep hidden in a box
even those who have no hope of hiding

We are taught that to acknowledge our complexity
is to ask to be excluded
It takes years to learn that this is their biggest mistake
That in our nuance lies strength

Disabled bodies are ecosystems
Our diversity unfurls a bridge to everything alive

Ceremony Traces the Root

I am not of the people of this place.
My ancestral lands occupied several miles from here
a canyon of stone boulders where birds feast on yucca
    pods
and ferns die, only to resurrect
to hundreds of miles away, paths etched up and across
    the span of the Americas.
      But with my umbilical cord buried here,
      mi cordón umbilical enraizado aquí,
      I am connected viscerally to this place.

To Greet Ancestors of Place

Orange dragonfly wings harmonize with my whispers
as its long body perches
on aloe flower stock hollowed and dried in desert
    sunlight
I have no idea if I do this right
A clumsy offer of respect
while knowing full well that the ancestors I speak to
are connected to people, resilient
powerful
engaged in honoring the messiness of community

I come to this spot from my city of squatters
Unresolved: treaties, sovereignty
and all it takes to uphold a colonial state
It feels brutal to digest
To acknowledge I live on stolen land, over and over, and
    over again
To not be able to fix it
To listen

To carry my own deep, embedded, sorrow
woven tight into the lines of my face
of my elders' dislocation from occupied ancestral lands

It is in this spirit of imperfection
in this unsatisfying reality built upon an invasive
    history of lies
as soft pinks cascade through the sky
brush my skin in the evening light
that I introduce myself through my lineages
and say, "Hello"

Benefaction

Great- \   Great- \   Great- \   Great- \
Great- \   Great- \   Great- \   Great- \
Grandmothers

Nanas, they go where I go
carrying these instruments of creation
womb, paintbrush, spirit, pen

Their song sings in my bones, whispers in my ear
I am and am not alone
Their song reminds me through my own grunts and
moans
of a spectrum of color to pull from as I paint a life

Burnt orange memory of daughter carried on mother's
back
Eyelids closed against the summer sun
Ache of splintered red heart strands, ties cut to lovers,
friends
Silver studded clarity which may come through prayer
or song, anger or betrayal, to fight for myself
Always flinging head-first into an infinite pitch-black
hope that both inner and outer journeys
are worth the risk

With golden truth that survival requires so much more
than any one person can do alone
Deliverance grows vivid green, like a new shoot of
alfalfa, after fallow times
A pink dab of humility reminds me that I am to Great
Spirit never too fierce or too much trouble

Three feathers inheritance tucked in my palette
shiver, quake with delicate strength
ready for ritual movement on canvas, on page

This color collection sung in my cells
stained in my blood
is of unequaled perfection

My
grandmothers
speak

The Rite of Home

I surrender
where gravity siphons
my heart

Here in the place of my blood
I only have slow visitors
ant, lizard, loud squawking raven
Grandfather Sun is vigilant in his attention
a luminescent brilliance
offers more questions than comfort

Too many leave their roots
scatter like seed to settle in cracks with like-minded
people

I too tried to find somewhere new until I discovered
there are no bats or big black bumble bees to covet my
nectar
I quickly wilted from too much water
Slumped slowly, returned to ground
There was not enough light or space to make me wonder
Fed all wrong, my creative juices squandered

I had to lose thorns, mountains
in order to discover I cannot

shake off the place where
tender points pierce sense of self
Where land maps the topography of my life

Now scarce water has taught me to embrace
gifts from sun, subtle ways to thrive
Cactus wren burrows into my side
heart flushed green to accept love from all sides

Here
I learn how to stay alive
Embody slow growth
wait for subtle drift of moisture
the monsoon clouds to gather
to shed most of my mass as I strive
Until patience is graced with flood of rain
A pliable welcome to expand roots deeper
fill veins with what is offered

Trunk instructs limbs to sprout leaves
bloom buds
drop fruit where I am

This tithing of sweetness
compels cycles
of revival

Found Feather Blessing

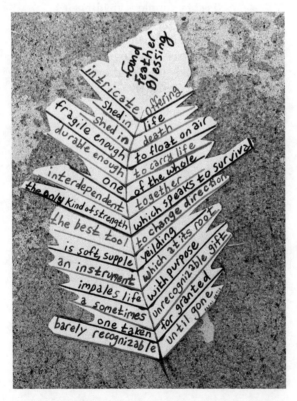

Fig. 3. "Found Feather Blessing" © 2021 Naomi Ortiz.

Picture description: poem text written in shape of a found feather

intricate – offering
shed in – life
shed in – death
fragile enough – to float on air
durable enough – to carry life
one – of the whole
interdependent – together
the only kind of strength – which speaks to survival
the best tool – to change direction
is soft, supple – yielding
an instrument – which at its root
impales life – with purpose
a sometimes – unrecognizable gift
one taken – for granted
barely recognizable – until gone

Ceremony Is Connection

Unfolding my chair, the legs crunch into the dirt as I sit down. Having slowly picked my way past ocotillos and triangle-leaf bursage, I settle in and notice a small saguaro, barely the height of my knee. It has survived its first forty years without getting trampled because it grew tucked under the twiggy limbs of a palo verde tree, where I am now sharing the shade. The tree is more protected from its namesake beetle who eats its roots because the saguaro's shallow root system spreads out over the surface area, slowing the beetle's access to the tree's roots. Survival of both plants is most noticeable on days like today when the saguaro's delicate flesh is plump, bright yellow flowers crowd through the palo verde tree's small leaves, and a kaleidoscope of tiny butterflies seek out the fragrant blooms between stem and thorn. This simple day-to-day support allows each plant to truly thrive.

My partner and I have been hanging out with a group of people who talk a lot about wanting to create community and a network of support. Thinking about how we could contribute to this shared vision, we had offered to host a meal celebrating the harvest season. We discussed with everyone what we were going to make — a main dish and the dessert, and asked others to bring side dishes. People agreed and seemed enthusiastic. My partner and I put in days of work to shop and prepare the dishes. On the day, folks showed up bringing very minimal contributions to the meal. About 45 minutes into the meal, several people announced that they were going dancing and needed to leave. I was really confused because I had communicated clearly about the expectation of shared mutual work and the creation of an opportunity to have discussion and fellowship. Instead of taking in the blessing of the harvest and allowing it spaciousness and attention, people opted for what was convenient, and without any communication, altered plans.

There are lots of times when I can only show up for an hour or contribute minimal effort to a shared event. Yet, if I commit to something, I prioritize my energy toward what I can do, including telling folks about changes. When I tried to talk to people about my experience of this dinner, people assumed my feelings were hurt because they didn't spend enough time with us. As we talked the conflict through, I realized that they viewed interdependence only as a rapid response in times of emergency, instead of gently tended relationships and small acts of care. This is like pointing to the flowers that bloom after a year of quiet mutual support and only then exclaiming, "This is what interdependence looks like!" If this is our understanding of interdependence, then when the urgency fades, so does the support.

> In nature
> giving and receiving
> both exist at once
> work in tandem
> Plants receive life-giving moisture from rain
> Javelinas eat nopal fruit with a ravenous appetite
> We receive
> the gift of our beating hearts pumping blood

without us ever asking
If we can't receive
we can't survive

I grew up observing interdependence between people – each weekend my mom and aunt swapping childcare. We shared food with my friends' families in the apartment complex we lived in. A human ecosystem of precarious survival.

After the first of many surgeries, I was rolled out from the hospital to our family car in a wheelchair with metal foot plates sticking out from the seat parallel to the ground. Both legs, from thigh to toe, were swaddled in thick heavy plaster casts. My parents and I discovered that because I was unable to bend my legs, there wasn't a way I could sit in the car. My mom went into problem-solving mode and located a family member with an old station wagon who offered to swap vehicles and let us use it. With help, I slowly transferred from my wheelchair, over the scratchy metal bumper, and slid into the cargo area. My wheelchair was disassembled, folded, and slung into the back seat. Over several more surgeries, this was how I got to doctor appointments and to the park to play with my cousins. I understood these big gestures as examples of how we made it through.

As a disabled adult, I have become deeply aware and appreciative of the small ways others support me to avoid institutionalization or group homes. I need help in order to survive. I've learned this exchange isn't always directly with the same person or equal in kind.

What does it mean to give and receive in bountiful but sometimes in inadequate or incomplete ways? Recently, I gathered up my courage and reached out to a friend for some help when I injured myself in a fall. She kindly agreed to vacuum my house. On the day we decided on, she had to cancel at the last minute.

However, she rescheduled and came the next week. During this same time, I volunteered to talk with an artist who had become disabled about how to navigate the waves of building and ebbing energy while still getting work done. The nature of interdependence means that we show up in support, when we can, in this larger ecosystem. The effort of give-and-take can be shared, passed around, between many people. Ideally, this means that care will be there in some form when it's needed, even if actions fall short, are piecemeal, or feel small.

What I've learned from watching interdependence unfold is that it doesn't leave relationships or family systems pristine. It is a random introduction of disruption, puts demands on our time and energy, and risks vulnerability. The thing about interdependence is that it requires sacrifice from both sides. It is a practice of both loss and of liberation.

Sacrifice can feel like a scary thing to consent to. We live in a world that extracts, demands, and takes. In our jobs, schools, and other social structures, competition means the same thing as participation. We do not get much practice consenting to a loss. Yet, if we want mutual liberation, then we need to be prepared for some loss of time, resources, energy, as well as a willingness to receive support. To have sources of support to turn to.

> Complex beings who both
> give and need help
> unfurl wings, sprout flowers, survive together

I have had my own process of learning, flipping back and forth between self-sacrifice or defending at all costs against any imposition. I needed to learn through trial and error about my own capacity. How to prioritize relationships without being taken advantage of or losing my own sense of goals and priorities. I've had to learn how to value a bit of conflict with others as we tried – sometimes succeeding, sometimes failing – to be there for each other. How this conflict was addressed determined whether or not a relationship could be interdependent.

The best interdependent relationships are built slowly. They may be with people I call friends, neighbors, or colleagues. A relaxed greeting to a neighbor, occasionally feeding their cat when they are out of town, or friendships built over coffee dates, giving a ride to the car repair shop, and working through disagreements, all quietly enrich the soil. Depending on the depth of the relationship, we put time into getting to know each other and having fun together. This builds trust to communicate when we need help or when we are unable to show up in the way the other person desires.

This faded sweater
unearthed in closet
Is borrowed, shared
Over time need arises to patch the rips, tears
Discover you have your ways of repair and I have mine
Learn, argue, listen
Pliable and soft
still takes tending

Interdependence is inherently inconvenient and through communication, it is also where limits and capacity can be respected. A beloved friend recently reached out for support during a mental health event when I had very low capacity. I told them this and affirmed that I cared about them. I asked if they could reach out to other folks, and then, if they couldn't find anyone else, to call me back. With time and laughter, as well as care, boundaries have been stitched into the fabric of this relationship. They trusted my capacity was not a reflection of how I felt about them. Later that evening I got a text that they were able to connect with another person and we sent each other some funny videos. This exchange uplifted my evening too. I checked in with them the next day.

I worry sometimes about being drained by providing help (or worry about being a drain to someone else by asking for help). Yet surprisingly, being there for others can be the best way to shake things up, get out of my own head, and have fun.

Interdependence is a dance with both disappointment and gratitude, but sometimes it comes with ease. One of the places I lived had a prolific grapefruit tree. When large yellow fruit swelled to gather in bunches between lush dark leaves, I would host juicing parties and my partner would bring boxes teeming with sweet-smelling fruit to his work. With more than we could use, abundance became necessary to share.

I have practiced interdependence with people and witness it in nature, but I am unsure how to be in relationship with the land in this way. Ecosystems are interdependent, but I never thought much about how humans fit into them. How I fit into them.

When I am discouraged, angry, or sad, I rely heavily on the land where I live for emotional support but feel at a loss to construct ways where I personally can provide it support. How can I be interdependent when I have so little say over what happens to the land? When my capacity to take physical action is so limited?

I reciprocate the best I can. Conserve water. Try to be mindful of packaging which will go straight into the dirt at the dump on the edge of town.

This all feels so passive. As a disabled person who needs to use resources, is it even possible for me to do enough to be beneficial? How do I give as well as receive?

As I sit under this vivid blue wide-open sky, I know the desert has never been "mine." I could never fully comprehend the intricate layers and beauty in even one patch. No, but I did – do feel like the desert claims me. I know that I am responsible to this place.

Ritual of Belonging

I got too close and pierced a vein
at the base of wrist on maguey's protruding spine
and we bled together
I belong to
dirt, that is stone broken down but not destroyed
sweat from the water I have the privilege to drink
the blue cloudless sky laughter
      each translation of my touch, taste, dream, inner sigh

I belong to
a conflicted community I cannot control
the swell, beat, truth of a melody both discordant and
    harmonic
my heart, both literally and metaphysically
loved ones who, like me, live with the consequences from
    both faults and glories
that rock, which cups my body like a chair, in the canyon
      where rattlesnakes tolerate my vibration

I belong to
breath exhale racing across desert sand
my ever-changing body, containing multitudes
ancestors who optimistically pledged life, blood, and bone
the stars above who get me drunk with perspective

Grandmother Moon, her face reflected back to mine
   each night with her gentle
      reminder that change is part of everything

Acceptance Is a State of Safe

Dry leaves snap off branches
like tiny shrapnel hurling through the air along with
    beetles and butterflies
all trying to navigate the churning torrent
The struggle to live is real

Wind breathes vitality into dust devil spirit
gathered from desert floor and sandy riverbeds
Twisters dance, swirl, for inches or miles
Between wispy, quickly moving clouds
Grandfather Sun beats down bright gaze
every agitated particle illuminated

I do not sit here unaffected on this picnic table
as I lean out over dry, deep, city wash
Dirt flies into eyes
wraps its way into hair
I am captivated by the challenge to brace body against
    wind
Earring flies sideways
threatens to be yanked from lobe

Next to this arroyo
birthing tiny cyclones of change
I imagine my sadness and longing

deftly gathered and pitched into this forceful movement
To watch fear, of life and death and everything in
    between
as it is carried, raging
Wind propels this anguish as it is swept up
dragged down
tumbling on and on
until
fury fully exhales

There, in my mind's eye
it rests cradled, naked to sky

                no one pays it any attention

There
    is calm
undisturbed and ancient

Peaceful enough for the dirt to drink distress down
    settle into safe

Rite of Mutual Attention

In the desert, I listen, plants speak
In the desert, I observe
plants show how to survive

In the desert, I let my guard down
plants sit patient
In the desert, I entrust the tender bits
plants are with me as I lay them down

I always ask permission:
to leave ragged and sharp remnants of a romantic
relationship beside a driveway in the generous pads of a
nopal cactus
to bury racist, ableist people in their own small
underground graves

                                    in my front yard
                                    on a rocky slope
                                    under an old oak tree
to leave unanswered questions and pain borne from an
imperfect parental relationship with dancing grasses
next to sandhill cranes who sing to each other as they
glide over the ephemeral water plain

I always acknowledge, always thank

Offer:
    kisses
    blood
    water
    hair
    song
    mutual regeneration

Ceremony Is Confrontation

This desert is where I burrow for shelter. Yet the cycles are shifting.

Temperatures soar higher, hotter, for longer. The heat offers only dust, a stillborn rain. Desert plants fold in on themselves, accordion flesh crinkled between thorns, as they use up water reserves stored.

Questions of reciprocity and interdependence uncover a deeper fear.

Can I witness the desert's slow death?

I have always felt responsibility to the desert, to the people of this place, but I have never felt like the land's need surpassed what I had to give. That it needed something outside of itself in order to live on.

I have never felt like it needed me to survive.

Portrait of Place

1990s

Sunlight glints off face through rear window

The back of my thighs sweat in black stirrup pants
against vinyl seats

Dust curls up behind us as we move slowly over
washboard road

Saguaros crowd the car sides surrounded by their
brethren chollas, magueys, ocotillos, mesquites

Desert spreads from under tire wheels, continuous into
background of mountains which jut upwards from valley
floor

When we pile out of the vehicle, there is nothing but
silence interrupted by occasional bird chatter

This place so far away from the city

Creosote seeds catch on wind, scent with rain

As my family wanders off on their hike

I sit on concrete bench, my body settles in

Belonging stretches in all directions

Present

2000s

Brow furrowed

I squint through sunlight as I navigate wheelchair van
over ever-deepening divots in dirt road

Flip cellphone doesn't have reception out here

Sidling up next to picnic bench on hardpacked dirt to
wheel across

His eyes open with awe as he enters one of my favorite
places backwards down ramp

Inspired by quiet, we sit, contemplate sun setting in sky

Secrets whispered drowned out by occasional car engine

The nopal stand, once thick, has turned brown, sunk
into the ground

Ocotillo still sprouts new limbs straight from
hardpacked dirt

Everywhere one looks

Cacti pose like nobility crowned with flowers

2010S

The engine chugs up the pass

Cresting the summit, almost on cue, sultry notes of Y La Bamba's "Moral Panic" begins to hum through iPod speakers

The desert I expect to see enveloping horizon

Interrupted by steady stream of dust as bulldozers scrape an ever-widening ribbon in the distance

Glimpse hundreds of bright reflections from glass windows before shifting attention back to narrow cliff hugging road

30 minutes later, I turn onto dirt path still as neglected as ever and steer around arroyo debris

Torn out plant matter surrendered to erosion carried downstream in the last storm

Settling on my bench, I greet spirit of my friend whose ashes now mix with the dust spread around this place we once sat

Nopal stand resurrected from what was once dead, shows off shiny new green pads

Lizard darts out from burrow underneath

Vibration of city trucks and trains, sound of traffic crowds in from a distance

Desert coexisting in patches still extends up into mountains

Distant ridge line goes flat, disrupted by man-made
removal before continuing its jagged, uneven dance

I lie back on picnic table surface to fill my eyes with sky

Ceremony Is Movement

Whenever I have felt powerless, I have always sought refuge in the desert to find grace. I am left feeling oddly abandoned. Deeply triggered. Can I bear the loss of my only safe haven?

Every day, flash flood warning
The only question is how fast the waters will rise

I have been avoiding the desert altogether. I cannot bear to fail it, and I do not know how to watch it slowly die. I don't know what I can do when there have been so many decades of extraction and abuse. How can I staunch the effects? I do not know if I am strong enough for any of this.

I have always gone to the desert when I feel this kind of despair but it has been months now. I finally decide that if I am truly in relationship with this place, then I need to ask what I can do.

I drive out to one of my favorite spots. A picnic area with concrete tables sprinkled over the slope side of national parkland. Turning down the dirt road, I pass towering saguaros stately watching over the land. New creosote bush limbs grow in a circle just outside dead branches which have bent to the ground. Green chollas so thickly covered in spines, only birds risk pecking at their fruit.

The wide blue sky is cradled between mountain ridges as I lie down on the picnic table to stare up into the vast universe. If I position my head just right, all I can see is sky and a smattering of clouds building near the horizon.

But I cannot get comfortable. So, I sit up on the table and stare out at the land sprinkled with this rich diversity of life. Under a large stand of nopales, a lizard shoots out from their burrow, headbutts dirt aside, seeking bugs. In the silences between a few twittering birds, I watch a tarantula hawk fly back and forth around the table where I sit. Its bright orange wings carry a thick black beetle body, attending to its tasks with devoted attention.

Grandfather Sun creeps higher. The skin on the back of my arms and neck starts feeling the scorch. I dig out my scarf to wrap around the back side of my body. Tourists pull up in their cars, like a parade of ants, to hike in the opposite direction from where I sit, to the crest of a hill dotted with petroglyphs carved into the boulders by the Ancient Ones. Hours pass and I do not know what to say.

Grandfather Sun slips behind the gathering clouds heavy with moisture. A rabbit hops by, its white tail the easiest to track as its dusty brown fur blends in with the ground. My shadow begins to lengthen into the surrounding cacti. I am still stewing in my anger and grief. A gust of wind twirls dirt into the air. Nearby an ironwood tree patiently rustles its gray limbs. The base of the tree splits into many trunks close to the ground. Each one solid and sacred as it opens itself up towards the sky. I wonder what it has seen in the centuries it has lived on this slope next to my bench.

I have been trying to hold my ground, but it finally dawns on me, there are never perfect words, only honesty. My scarf pulls at my throat as a crack of lightning announces rain. I start in – blabbering about how guilty I feel, that the care of this land feels too big. I tell the cacti, trees, and dirt that I do not want to resent this place of comfort. I do not know if I am strong enough. The wind carries my words off into the heart of the desert.

Continuing on I start voicing questions like, "Can I still ask and seek support from this place? Is my need too much?" Silence answers. Then the sudden rattle and pelt of downpour. Tourists shout as they scramble to their cars.

My clothes are plastered to my skin. I yell into the storm, "How the hell do I support you in this time of devastation?" My body emptier from sharing my worries and questions, I surrender to the rain and listen.

After treacherous torrential release
I am no longer drowning

Sunlight breaks through a crack in the clouds. Some of the rays are blocked by the mountain ridge far to the west. The rain slows as quickly as it came. In the subsiding light and returning heat, I hear from the sky, from deep down in my chest, from the soil,

Love Harder.
Be part of the web of those who love place.

Love harder... I am elated! I can do love.

The breeze picks up and joins me in my deep sigh of relief.

Leaving through the settling darkness, I feel so grateful to be heard and answered. An answer that is appropriate to me and what I can do. My heart sings and I hum along as I watch the road for mule deer, javelinas, and coyotes. Driving through the darkening silhouettes against the fading sky, I start really thinking about it.

What does it actually mean to love harder?

Interlude 2

Sitting outside, a new friend and I chat on the porch. Hummingbirds zoom in and hover drinking down the food I have carefully funneled into the feeder. I notice as we chat that the feeder is looking empty and comment that I need to make more food. My friend pauses and stares off into the distance.

I admire her homemade snack, her scent unsmothered by deodorant. Smooth skin the color of clay. Who loves on whomever tempts her eye, who spends her time catching babies. She is the epitome of *got her shit together*, this kickass woman. Her organic, vegan, yoga-toned, nondisabled body glistens in the late afternoon light.

Her gaze slides to mine as she asks if I use white sugar to make the hummingbird's food. "Yeah," I answer hesitantly. Her face is impassive, but something in her eyes hardens. "Colonizers got our communities hooked on sugar and it has contributed to our destruction and our addictions," she states matter-of-factly. "I worry about giving any creature white sugar."

I feel punched in the gut, both with the truth of this, and by my confusion. Was I making the hummingbirds sugar addicts? Was I poisoning hummingbird communities with my sugar-water good intentions? Didn't this white sugar liquid food help keep them alive?

And yet, wasn't that what our communities have been told as we drown in food deserts where packaged food substitutes for real food?

I take a deep breath and allow a small smile. Sometimes we can be so tough on each other.

To Be Part of the Web of Those Who Love Place

When in fear, I aim for safety.
  As a disabled person of color, my body, needs, and perspective do not have a home in conventional responses to climate change. Dismantling systems that were built up over centuries to increase access to the resources I rely on for food, shelter, and connection is not the strategy I choose. When the task is taking apart something layered that I use to provide for every necessity, the work of this feels incomprehensible.

Where is safety in this time?
  Is it in the ways I find to shore up my own security?
  Is it in voting and giving my proxy to corporations to make the changes needed?
  I am not sure.
  What I do know is what a pursuit of safety is not. It is not going zero waste. I can't reuse bandages. My hand does not pinch four fingers to thumb, elbow cannot bend, in order to insert menstrual cup. I bleed too fast, too heavily for cloth pads. Waste equals function.

Safety is not found in growing my own food. Choices have to be made about how my energy is used. Everyday there is a finite amount. Do I use that energy to water and tend the soil, or do I use that energy to make meals and clean myself? As a disabled person, self-sufficiency is never viable for survival.

I feel like a lost soul wandering around the communities and discourses of the environmental movements. Shaking my jangly earrings, whispering, "Hello" into the wind. My ghostly presence one they cannot quite make out.

Yet, they use language in which I recognize my reflection.

Mining scars cripple and deform the earth. People are blind to the cost. Pollution spreads like a cancer.

Disabled bodies are thrust like a dam to make people stop and pay attention. Using the fear of my body and other disabled people's bodies as a metaphor for environmental destruction, is just using fear to incite fear.

Fear of disability is transferred and leveraged as a cautionary tale, to stop us from embracing our environments.

Why incite more fear? Does fear create agency? Because I can tell you, fear does not define my relationship to my disabled body.

Discrimination? Fewer options? Yes.

Making do with less? Making hard choices? Yes.

But I have an intimate awareness of my needs. I know what minimums I can live on.

Here it is — we now live in a disabled world. Earth has been forever altered.

Disability is not fair. Some of us live shorter lives.
Some of us do not make it. Some of us live far better
and longer than anyone would have predicted.
There is not a road map for change, but change is
happening.

I, too, want to save ecosystems. I believe the animals
and plants deserve to live. Yet if disability has taught
me anything, it has taught me there is much I do not
control. Very little in fact. But choices always matter.
Disability is a life of inhabiting contradiction and
venturing into vulnerable unpredictability.

A foundational element of ableism is a fear of
vulnerability.
    If one is afraid of being vulnerable, how does one
    adapt?
    In the Sonoran Desert, the palo verde tree has green
    bark in order to absorb sunlight, so it is free to
    shed its tiny leaves during long periods of drought.
    Vulnerability is the best teacher of adaptation.
    Disabled people know that living into the future
    means learning to ask for help. To be patient,
    flexible, and insistent. Helping each other is not
    always convenient and we can respect our own
    capacity. Boundaries can also exist. Grappling
    with interdependence is slowing down. Listening.
    Disappointing each other and mending.

Disabled people know how to adapt to a world which is
ever changing without considering us.
    I have touched the edges of interdependence. I
    know how underdeveloped and limited people's
    understanding of interdependence is. Yet climate
    change is not an "I" situation. Actually, if it were just
    up to me, fine, I would do it. But as a single person
    against the proposal of the world's largest copper

mine or the housing developments that keep getting constructed despite the lack of groundwater, I can only do so much. Relying on each other, however, builds power.

Climate change is a "we" situation. We have hard choices to make. To flourish, we must consider accessibility and interdependence in relationship to everything.

What interventions can support continued life? How can they be sustained? By whom?

Where do we need to just accept the altered state? How do we adapt?

Ask for help?

How do we prepare not just for suffering, but for sharing and innovation?

These questions are not just full of agency and self-determination, they are what hope looks like now.

My Sphere of Influence

My world is hot sizzle sweat drip on sleeve

My world is mint green walls yielding to windowpane

My world is collage of dictation software typing on
computer screen – correcting *in* to *and* – cobalt blue
paint smeared where forearm touched canvas, and
stools in every room on which to perch so I do not
have to stand

My world is coffee or tea sipped from sparkly wonder
woman underwear cups and pottery thrown mugs,
deep, deep

My world is community care collective meetings, zoom
chats with self-care seekers, loud laughing phone
calls with friends

My world is sitting next to me on this porch swing
swatting away mosquitoes

My world is dirt that blooms deep shades of red and
brown wherever raindrops complete their journey
from cloud to ground

My world is cactus thorns catching fire-bright as sun
sets until snuffed out with the fading light

My world is watching young ones on TV, brave bodies
clad only in cloth, swarm cities with signs Black Lives
Matter

My world is cooking frozen mushrooms with greens
plucked from clear plastic bag

My world is music, always on background, foreground,
Big Mama Thornton, Calexico, Nina Simone, Jaguar
Wright, Ojos de Brujo, Puccini, Ozomatli, Rage
against the Machine, Los Cojolites, The Cure

My world is nightly reading of *What the Fuck Just
Happened Today?*,[1] picking one outrage, writing
representatives

My world is texting about the day-to-day with beloved
twenty-year-old in her first apartment

My world is taming kitten claws with soft skin, boiling
water for hummingbird food, listening to wind

My world is missing a loved one that I couldn't pry loose
from the cycles of addiction

My world is fixing water leaks

My world is swallowing fear of tomorrow shaken out by
tremors that crack apart everything today

My world is plugging things in and unplugging them

1   Matt Kiser, *What the Fuck Just Happened Today?*, https://
whatthefuckjusthappenedtoday.com/.

My world is small yet consumes all my attention

The Topography of a Small Place

Have I ever really known the dirt spread at my feet? Contour leans, curves, dips, rises. Going on seven years here and I know only basic shape, square. Where the trees are, mostly. But the dirt, I only engage when weeds appear. Thick growth. Volunteers of the annoying kind. Yank! Sweat trickles down forehead, springs over eyebrow, leaps into eye, sashays down jawline, drips onto soil. This is the only tribute, the only thing I give, along with an occasional drag of the hose over to root span to trickle meager offerings to this land on top of which I live.

The Topography of a Small Place

Love as Refuge
Part 1

Loving harder. What does this actually mean? This question zooms and circles in my mind, like a turkey vulture hunting for its next meal, until I slowly begin to panic.

One day I found myself driving through an area of town where I grew up. Sagging wooden fences with rotted posts, weeds thick through barren lots, but also, apartment balconies stuffed with precarious pots of lovingly tended succulents. It made me remember that through my teen years I tried to use love like a tool. Loving harder became a tactic to respond to abuse and dysfunction. When people in my life withdrew, I would "love harder." Show up, try to be steady, reliable.

We grew wild
Tangled in survival
Refused to be pruned
We let go as we must
The first punch was never the last

When, especially as a young adult, people in my life treated me badly, I paid attention to their subtle reactions and body language. I did this in order to adjust, to be as close as I could to what they indicated they wanted me to be.

A tingling on my neck
Practiced at quick glance
skilled read of situation
On guard when others are relaxed

Somewhere along the way I convinced myself that if I could just love the person harder, I would pierce through harm, and shift the relationship to one of mutual love.

As a disabled young person, so much of the social exclusion I faced was framed by occupational therapists, teachers, and other authority figures, as me not trying hard enough to fit in. I could feel what was happening behind my back before I saw with my eyes. A kid lurching side-to-side mimicking my walk while the other kids around us laughed. When I was bullied, these adults instructed me to not let how young people reacted to my difference dissuade me from being their friend.

The awful thing was, sometimes it worked. I would prove myself or push back in a way where I was included — sort of. I could eat lunch with these kids I had won over as friends by sheer tenacity but was rarely invited over to their house. Being flexible and adapting automatically to shifts in other's behaviors and moods helped me survive as a child, and continue to serve me as a disabled person living in an inaccessible and ableist society.

Validate their understanding
of time
of what makes a good life
Play the game
Truth is precious — hide

Dispossess signs of disagreement
To them inclusion is a noun, not a verb

I pulled out the "loving harder" tool in many
relationships which revolved around the other person's
needs, errands, and priorities. I'd give money I had
scrimped and saved to friends who reluctantly told me
it would help but never said, "Thank you." Loving harder
evolved to constantly worrying if I was proving myself
worthy of love. At its most insidious, it left me feeling
obsessive and acting overly responsible for others. Tying
my safety to the question, *"Am I doing enough to be loved?"*
There is no winning at trying to be enough for others.
By positioning my worth based on how other people
were or were not happy with me, I gave them control. If
I wasn't available when others wanted my company or
help, if I asserted my need to get groceries, do laundry,
or work on art, they would ignore my calls for days. I'd
love harder, worry, keep calling, apologize, and at the
next opportunity jump at their invitation, regardless
of what I had planned. There was always a part of me,
deep down, that knew this felt wrong. A part of me that
resisted.

You ask me to conjure a miracle
like divinity follows me home from your house
my forgotten bolero wrapped around its shoulders
I can only light a candle in this mystery
that's all I dare

I would practice by standing up for my rights
or setting boundaries with people whom I wasn't
dependent on. In this way, I have learned. When I was
ready, I created boundaries where I needed to and
grieved the losses of those who could not engage with
me in an honest and vulnerable dialogue about how we
treated each other.

This love was always tricky
more a source of endurance than bountiful
My cheekbones, your lips
everything which made us unique
beheld in our friendship
observed without statement
Your dark eyes hover over
glass liquor bottle radiant in the glint of dawn
We live in alternate realities
made toothed by addiction and boundaries

My adult years have been spent unlearning the toxic belief that trying harder will get me what people are actually unwilling to give. I have come to redefine love as investing in time, patience, and honesty. To trust relationships which grow slowly and take years to deepen with people who care about my needs as much as I do theirs. I have changed my definition of love to mean giving myself as much as I give others.

The desert is a diverse and intricate ecosystem. My relationship with it is not like a person. Yet, still I worry about becoming obsessive.

I cannot quite figure it out.

This idea of loving harder circles around and around in my head. What action does it require? What do I have to do?

Loving. Harder.

I love fully and deeply. I am all in. Loving is not the problem. Love means care, attention, witnessing, sacrifice, and compromise. Loving sometimes means accepting less but enjoying it more. But the desert is not just asking for my love, it is asking for me to love harder.

To Accept Where I Am

In this state of in-between is both silence
and   the   screech of longing

Asked daily to get over their mistakes made in ignorance
Never ready with bated breath answers for the
questions they ask
or prepared with stories to remind them of what they
already know
Worked hard to forget friction of desire to feel
understood
Persist in a vacuum of belonging

Instead, a melody of music is what I pin my hopes on
That someday, somewhere, someone will just sit back
and listen
Let my chorus of voices reclaim the multitude of ways to
yearn, grieve, rejoice

Cause amongst my ribs, spleen, and heart
I live in an emptiness crowded by caterpillars inching in
determined directions
I nurse wounds which, when kindled
ignite baggage from the past

I make room for ancestors who slaughtered each
other, who ran from decimation, who benefited from
annihilation

This body born backwards, turning inside out
spills menstrual blood onto the carpet
lurches as movement
demands change just to get in the door
is still unsure how to protect the bits exposed

In between sacrifice and gift
I make a home in
a canyon which leads only back into itself
through split, circle, rocky existence
It makes sure
I learn everything's name, as part of my name
This spiral canyon which claims me
teaches me patience
a kind of truth without resolution

Interlude 3

A cooper's hawk shadow sweeps across the hood of my vehicle as I pull onto the patch of dirt before the concrete surface of the carport. Out of the corner of my eye I see something dart from a desert shrub up and away. Later, returning from the grocery store, I again see quick movement as my vehicle rumbles up past the same bush. Curious, I wander over to look in amongst the skinny limbs. There, a woven collection of city-grown pine needles, small twigs, and feathers are perched. Shaped like the tiniest teacup on top of a limb barely able to carry its weight, yet, securely attached by spiderweb. Each time I've pulled in or out of the drive, a hummingbird has dashed away scared from her nest.

Disability access is tough enough carrying in lightly loaded bags from the grocery store. There is not much room to park on the street, but somewhere deep inside I feel stubbornness arise. The noise from my vehicle scares this hummingbird away from their nest. This little feathered creature, who could fit in the palm of my Crip hand, with a bright orange bill, was somehow finding a way to bring new life into this world. I wanted to support.

I convince my partner it is worth the trouble in order to make room for this small family and we start parking as far as we can without scaring the little hummingbird who now sits upon her egg in the nest. Late afternoon I return from a grocery trip. A trickle of sweat rolls down the side of my face as I haul a 5 lb bag of rice through my front door. "This is such an inconvenience!" I whine and then startle my partner as I start laughing because my next thought is to wonder if the mama hummingbird also thinks this about my racket as I squish and maneuver plastic bags by her. *This is what interdependence looks like,* I remind myself. *Sometimes inconvenient but doable.*

I try to keep a respectful distance but as the days stretch into weeks, I keep an eye out for changes. One day, while watering my little potted herb garden, I notice a strange new shape in the nest. What looks like a tiny twig sticking up from the inside rests against the rim.

Hummingbird Legacies

Baby lies prone
almost too small to see
Eyes closed
Claws move of their own accord
The goal is to just breathe

Slung inside half-marble-sized nest
tiny body surrenders to curve of support
slick head connects long beak

Not yet ready
to spread feathered wings
No muscles yet
to move them at their 70+-per-second beat

I worry about baby as the wind flings
thin tendril of branch every which way
but mama has faith
in anchor strength of stolen spider web

Baby lays prone
eyes not quite open
Does not know the dangers of this place
on the edge of the world
the span between my carport and the neighbors'

Outside
mama squeaks and chirps in my direction
Reminds to refill feeder
it is not just her

I wonder what dangers lurk
Arms and chest itch to
protect
do more

But mama knows
all life is just a legacy
of vulnerability

Love as Refuge
Part 2

Days turn into weeks as I spin out on what *harder* means for me. Finally, at an impasse, I realize that I need to go back to the desert and ask. I drive through traffic up into the mountain range north of town, to a trailhead where I can look straight up into mountain canyons. It is late morning and the heat is increasing. I perch on a rock next to the parking lot. This is as far as I can go, but I let my eyes drift over the saguaros standing thick, arms mostly pointed toward the sky and their desert plant companions covering the mountainside.

A jojoba bush near my arm starts shaking as a small brown bird forages within its limbs. I sit in the bright baking silence, a raven flies by, sky walking. My mind wanders as I watch the ants blaze trails over and under the rock I am sitting on. I pray for a bit of a reprieve as I shift to stay out of their way. *Diversity can be so distracting, inconvenient,* I think and simultaneously laugh at myself and how human I am to be inconvenienced by the creatures of the place where I also seek refuge.

I whisper my fears to the mountainside, I wait for a reply. I think through the costs of *loving harder* in my life. How it often felt like a precursor to denial rather than a fruitful act. Sweat starts to trickle down my back and I brush wayward ants off my legs. I know I need to move on, continue with my day.

I hold a spark of fear in my heart that there will be no new information. I zone out on the rocky boulders jutting sideways from the ridgeline. From the mountainside, from deep within my body, I hear,

We see each other.
We are <u>with</u> each other.

So, loving harder as... *being with*.

Witnessing with attention.

I have long contemplated the dicho, "¿Y dónde está tu ombligo?" A saying literally translated as, "Where is your bellybutton?" But the dicho means, "Where are you centered or rooted?" How do I witness when the place I feel rooted to is in distress?

Witnessing requires a long-sustained relationship.

Being with means one has to be there.

As a disabled person of color, I do have some well-developed skills for witnessing. In the process of grappling with not being accepted, I have stayed with the experiences, witnessed the effects of both cruelty and neglect through my body and heart. The literal lack of access to move about, to go where I want, has taught me to appreciate where I can go, to notice where I am.

Driving down from the mountain back toward home, I struggle with doubt. Do I have the emotional stamina to withstand witnessing unprecedented changes within an ecosystem, much of which may not live in the way it has before?

I do have a choice.

I could instead shut down, turn away, focus on man-made surroundings I can control. But. But I need the desert as much as it needs me. *We see each other...*

That night I write my representatives and senators about contractors building Trump's border wall. The administration disregarded environmental and water protection laws in drilling out millions of gallons of groundwater and endangering one of the only freshwater places in the desert, Quitobaquito Springs. O'odham and other people, as well as animals, have depended on this water source, that we know of, for 16,000 years. The endangered Quitobaquito pupfish and the Sonoyta mud turtle, who has also been deemed a candidate for protection under the Endangered Species Act, along with other plant and animal species, are threatened from this careless usage of water.[1]

We see each other.

Somehow the water table dropping to dry up the only freshwater spring in the Sonoran Desert seems achingly symbolic. A couple of weeks later I get letters back on the congresspeople's stances on the border wall. No mention of Quitobaquito Springs. No mention of the groundwater table dropping. The denial of something precious cannot help but bring up so much grief. *Being with*, I am learning, is grief work.

---

1   "Quitobaquito Springs," *National Park Service,* June 24, 2018, https:// www.nps.gov/orpi/learn/historyculture/quitobaquito-springs.htm.

Witnessing Is Grief Work

Witnessing is intimate. To hover as burrows are
unearthed. Be showered in dirt, gasp alongside for air.
It is more than observing, more than watching.
I am affected by what I witness – I am not disconnected
from land, neighbor, bird, lizard, city, friend, world.

Witnessing is deep heart work.

Witnessing is shattering open spirit work.

Witnessing is despair work.

Witnessing is to touch vulnerability. To sit uncomfortable
with pounding palpate of more and more extreme. A
friend talks to me of what makes her want to end it all.
Out here in the wild wonder of life, weighed down by
fear of landlords, ex-lovers. I sit present, like I do with
the ocotillo leaves turning brown from the long-ago
rains.
I want sufficient ways to help but this misery isn't
tended by my goals. It is soothed by open heart being
alongside messy truth and complication.

Witnessing is prayer work. Desperate clutch and hold
clammy hands with the feeling of powerlessness.

That the wildfires will burn out. Animals find refuge and
do not suffer. Plants have protected roots — fire misses
some of the seedlings.

That Black, Indigenous, Brown, Trans, Disabled,
Immigrant bodies will be valued.

That the crack to reimagine elder care will widen to
shift everything. That disability community will take
our place at the forefront, in partnership with others, to
dream additional alternatives for how support and care
happen.

Am I sending fear? More trauma energy? Guilt? Sadness?
It is completely fine to feel these things, but am I being
careless with where I place these emotions?
How am I purposefully attending to what I feel?
Faith is a fist made of many fingers – strength found in
bracing against each other.

Witnessing is altar work. I let the essence of events find
me in rocks, water, seeds. To call to my heart through
the mundane and allow experience to be contained.
        My altar is my space, a visual representation of this
moment in life.
I wipe away dust, check if the rocks need cleansing. Or, if
I am too frazzled, I trust what is there. Place tablespoons
of precious water and let my fear, disgust, and sadness
float up. I light candles and give permission for my
tangle of emotions to rest on gray and rose-colored
rocks.
This is an appropriate place to work with what I feel. A
container that cannot break.
I immerse, recede, respect the flow of need.

To witness is to be an apparition, leave little evidence
and a memorable

presence. Preserve testimony.

Witnessing is compassionate clarity, a bird's eye view.
Utilize distance to back out to see the stitches from
those who have picked up thread and scissors, who have,
many times, sewn the world back together — mended
but changed. Altitude assists in designing an adapted
future.

Witnessing is to consume history. To listen deeply to
generations of people who have labored imperfectly
toward crafting alternatives to the racist, ableist,
capitalist world we live in.
Who in their times of transformation, traced the
patterns from their elders for knitting ourselves into
unfamiliar ways of being community.

Witnessing is reciprocity in its most non-transactional
form.
At a community potluck an unhoused woman
stands in the middle of everything, the story of how
her son died propelled by each breath. Wails between
the words. This room of witnesses does not register to
her until one person sets their plate down on the floor,
perching their fork on its rim just so, walks over, and
asks to embrace her. Only then, can the mother eat.

Witnessing is action, a fierce swing of light.
Deeds propel us into the future but also bleed backwards
into the past.
A circulation of grace.

In the unsteady pace of waves of energy, time, try
to answer: How am I supporting what is collectively
being requested? What am I asking for within my own
communities? What do I feel called to do from my

intuition, from the universe? How am I continuing to
listen? To witness?

Into the Noise

Running late
Red brick buildings
swarm above my head like a pack of hungry buzzards
eagerly watch as I drive
They crowd in, block the sunshine

Duck into luminous cave-like opening
whose entrance provides momentary cover
in this dark and gloomy early morning light

Structure dull gray, cold, squeaks of
rubber tires making tight turns
Flash of headlights dodge between
pressed suits and jingling keys
we all keep circling, ascending
until I find open space
Windshield looks out at tops of trees
Here wind moves free

The others' rhythms – quick exit from vehicle
gather jackets, bags, swift to wait for elevator
My rhythm is different – slide of legs out door
slow move to unload scooter
rest
Except for my nervous heart

beats on this side of fast
Nervous worry about this morning's meeting
but wait
there it is again

Shhhh.... I hold my breath and listen

Radial high note blasted like a tiny trumpet
wrecks quiet dawn, tone then drops low
before trilling back up in scale
guttural *Rrrrr,* rolled with sass

The song begins over
of a bird no bigger than my finger
that I extend to touch the tip of my lower lip
awed by the curious recognition
of joy

Somewhere, camouflaged in manicured landscape
these sweet notes
echo between floors
rise up through the cracks into brilliant blue sky
both showing off at 7 AM

Serenaded as I slowly connect
pieces of scooter, she is ready to roll
to move me on sidewalk poured long ago
to a building three blocks from here

Push elevator button
as small creature poetry
rises above
concocted importance

Permeates throughout this concrete structure
this bastion of human innovation
vibrating with the business of human existence

Hummingbird's melody dances around me
as my spirit remembers the pleasure of singing into the
    noise

Besieged

There is   no   taking   her   down
          Summer
Comes one day, full force
Spits out yellow petaled flowers dusted red
Tosses, lands, like a brick of hot swirling wind

My sweat pays tribute
to her demand to
yield
burrow   survive

Summer unleashes in a fiery assault
Dust mixed pollen fresh
Brings water to eyes, mucus to nose
Life flees to the shade
to practice acceptance as she settles in
Bright, fierce, swallows up all blue sky
Desert flesh undeterred by abundance of heat
ready to receive what sun gives
without pomp of bark, frill of leaves
just thorns to deter any who mistake utility for
fragility
Here, survival is high art

Go deep
down
through throat to chest
nuzzle density
locate cool
in this rocky soil cracked skin
lie flat
front to ground
Wait the day out

Interlude 4

Over the block fence doused in shadow, my neighbor's chili pepper lights briskly strobe on and off, highlighting their backyard and bushes in a weak red light before it plunges back into darkness. The outdoor lights have been strobing for weeks now, since a storm came through, causing the electronic current to become erratic. I steel myself for tolerating the disco atmosphere for the next couple of months until the neighbor's return.

Leaving for the summer to avoid the desert heat is a privilege I sometimes envy on nights like tonight when the sweltering air is coated with thick humidity. The monsoon season, a fifth season in the Sonoran Desert, is one that many of us who call this place our home, look forward to. A friend refers to it as "the mon-swoon," because in a matter of hours an intense storm builds up from behind one of the mountain ranges. One learns to somehow endure 115° heat by anticipating the sharp crack of thunder and streaks of lightning; the wind stirring the atmosphere into a peak moment before the climax of rain. Release comes when large drops hurtle from the sky and pound into the land. Soil absorbs what it can, before the ground turns into flowing sheets of water, sliding to the lowest points, gathering into raging rivers, barreling down normally dry arroyos. Sensational storms leave everyone with stories of harrowing efforts to not be washed away or with joyous squeals about the immediate 20° drop in heat.

This year, the storms never came. There have been a few, but most of this season is like tonight. The humidity moved in, the wind kicked up swirling the dirt and twisting small leaf and thorn-covered limbs in impossible directions, only to slowly calm and fade away.

Hot does not describe the sticky warmth radiating through the air, plastering every surface to my skin. The ground heaves a long sigh of heat.

Climate change. Each new story of massive shifts affecting all of us creatures impales my body deeply with pangs of fear and stress about the nature of our survival. I have known about the possibility that this time was coming since I was a kid watching *Captain Planet and the Planeteers* desperately trying to save humanity from itself. This is a fear I have always held at arm's length as I hoped regulation and environmental protections could corral us back into safety. But here we are.

I fall back and forth between lapses of terror or trying to act on what I can. What has surprised me about being alive at the precipice of unalterable change to how, where, and what life looks like, is the grief. I worry about being swallowed alive by grief. The truth is, I struggle with this possibility daily, from my toes to my head. I am nothing but a part of where I live.

This deliberate web of life rooted everywhere is designed to take advantage of exactly where it is. Centuries of persistence and creative propagation have made a densely woven desert. Watching small shock waves of catastrophe has become a billowing, seeping numbness.

These changes can feel like jumps and starts, but mostly it is slow. A gradual decrease in how many Couch's spadefoot toads burrow in the soil waiting to come alive in the rains, to the creeping spread of invasive buffelgrass, which, once lit, wipes out in a heartbeat plants that have lived for hundreds of years.

I grasp at this reality through a tempest of terror and despair. What does it mean to live here? Now? In a storm that is always building. Building in pressure, and in force – while sitting in this awful discomfort is where I pray, I stay, because I do not know how to survive the release.

How I can maintain my life staring into the face of these changes?

The stars twinkle in the vast sky. Dark outlines flash in and out of my view as the neighbor's neglected lights preview the chaos to come.

Ritual for Courage

When I need courage, I draw plants

Like safety can be quantified in drawing, therefore
knowing, weeds which grow in my yard, at the side of
the road, in the arroyo

In this dry gritty dirt where I sit, life springs up
unadorned where animal or wind dropped seed
                        amidst everything

Pencil lines arch, friction of hand slides over page,
shakes loose what scares me

As shape becomes form, confidence is inspired by stems
flung open wide to sun
Leaves bend in flow of breeze, relax, give themselves
some room

> *Tiny flowers at the end of long peduncle*
> *Entire plant, smooth to the touch*
> *Blue-green leaves notched at the margin*
> Later, learn: *Leaves edible, medicinal herb*
> *Papalo Quelite*

A practice to learn the secrets behind a name

Fortitude unearthed by greeting what lives at my feet

Change Escalates

Left shoulder blade aches
Side body does not want to be stretched
Sit conclave toward window
Stomach churns acid
Mind tries to take charge, attempts to straighten spine
yet to pull shoulder blades back feels altogether too
    vulnerable

So I distract my disappointment
by neck roll
       right sideways tilt ear to hover above shoulder
           view of dusty porch light
       drop chin to chest
           fuchsia pink lightning bolt drips down panza
       roll up, left jaw bone inches past collar, right ear
       listens to sky
           watch hummingbird feeder swing in hot, dry
           breeze
middle back muscles pull attention, ache

In the distance
milky plumes rise from behind thick stretch of
    mountains carved by steep valleys

Connected by eyes, heart tightens throat
hope for clouds
but instead accept smoke

Pelvic bone tries valiantly to hold
the mess of me
sitting here helpless
seeking calm by noticing

Unknown

1.

Tongue licks air – smoke
is a taste, a smell
Invokes fear, raises hackles
Is there anything to do but move away?
Burrow in my shell
watch out the window
as gray plumes rise from mountain ridge
Fire spins around the peaks
twirls downward, pirouettes
closer

2.

Desert does not burn
Green thorn-laced skin
plump from short storm bursts
Moisture patiently gathered
from superficial roots
Reliant on inhospitable
Depends on toughness
carefully honed survival

Palo verde with thin green limbs
to photosynthesize light
no need to rely on its small leaves
easily shed in tribute
to a cloudless sky

Kangaroo rat tucks found seeds
left for months, years
under unrelenting desert sun
in cheek pouches hydrate tough dry
reconsume the moisture as it chews softened kernels

Ocotillo grows series of
thorn-covered sticks from
one root bundle
taller than a house
Lives for a hundred years
Knows when to grow leaves
When to let them go
People cut stalks
plant for fence and still
they live no matter the place
A waterfall of crisp pink or maybe orange flowers
clustered in cones nestled together cascade from their
    tips

Without water
leaves are a luxury
Beauty blooms, however, are essential

3.

These adaptations develop slowly
take time
Fire is nothing but fast
Tears across hillsides, consumes
snuffs life out of existence

Fire loves the fuel we have brought
buffelgrass, dandelion weeds
We share our greed, it burns hotter
stands back on hind legs, pushes upward
tower twenty-foot flames
swallows all plants in its way

Our desert burns

4.

After the smoke fades
when fire has eaten enough
to let itself be contained

The after is beginning

Too rapid of a shift for animals to remain
My structure in the middle of the city is safe

Left to hope for
seeds buried, glanced over
time to reassert steady
faith to pitch future forward beyond my lifetime
the patience of four generations to regrow
to become a semblance of before

We all grieve in our own way
With the rains, soil lets go, surrenders, washes away
Some people
pretend it does not affect them
hike old paths forever changed
Others
focus full hearted
on silhouette and pray

32.378 Latitude – 110.943 Longitude

Mountain range
rolls the length of my body
where I planted my feet, teenage angst alone
watched world split open to orange sunsets
west wind ignited passion, heart to dream
                                        To the other end
            where I accompanied my niece on her first entry into
                                                        pine forest
                                getting dirty climbing boulders
                                    to disappear behind ridgeline
                            Mountain range
middle where I placed a photo of my grandmother's face
encased in a metal star made from an aluminum can in
that lost chapel, the most honest religious place, roof
                        slit open to let in sky
                        Before the intrusions
                    bits and pieces scraped away
            my body remembers where love existed
between maguey flower stalks and saguaro night blooms
A desert church with stone floors and plaster painted
                                    walls
            where my mom and dad, grandparents, aunties,
                                gathered
                        to witness wedding vows
                    which also dissolved in smoke

        Still, a home for the glimmer of me
Mountain range
steady steward to my left cascading east
Wild comfort
secure in never being tamed

This fire
an indicator

In the dark, made its own light
traveled the ridge
devoured valleys for miles
combustion inescapable
Now charred soil, the smoke still uncoils
lightning sparked forever change

120,000 acres, seven weeks in
Hundreds of thousands of gallons of pink poison, aerial
    dropped
splattered like fear graffiti
Panic adds another thing which cannot be undone
but the mansions remain

How is beauty reclaimed?
Will the profound density of diversity
ever be the same?

All I can do is sing to soothe
Refamiliarize myself with the body of home

After the fire
I am a microclimate of faith

Love as Refuge
Part 3

I can still feel the steam baking up off the charred ground as I sit in the 112° heat. My drive out to be with the land cut short by closures due to the fire. I get as close as I can before the cresting upward push of mountain body and park to the side of a water tank and barbed wire fence. The arroyo is puckered, parched, filled only with sand and trash. Mesquite limbs drape, swish, back and forth sawing in soft grind on slats of an old wood fence cradled by a tangle of plastic chair parts. Yet even with this discarded debris, where I sit is still lush in comparison to the swaths of black nothing that trace haphazardly from my side of the mountain, up, over the top, and down into the valley on the other side.

We see each other.
The shock reverberates on my skin.

Weeks later I return. Grief still thick in my eyes, heart heavy. Able to access now the parking lot for rugged hiking trails, I sit on a rock perched between people-claimed and wild. I stare up into the depths of the hidden canyons, unseen but affected and felt. A protein bar wrapper flicks and crinkles as it is swatted across the pavement by the warm breeze.

I feel tethered to a yearning for restoration and imagine fuchsia pink flowers sprouted on cholla, surrounded by many bushy creosote limbs draped with tiny puffball seeds making the air smell like the sweet bouquet of rain. Replacing in my mind *what is*, the scalded earth torn away, with what I wish it would be, the desert existing just as before, is compelling because it releases me from now. Here.

Being here means I am pitched headfirst into the depths of my despair at being unable to do anything. I find myself saying to the mountains, *I am so sorry.*

I am so,   so   sorry.

Suddenly, from the inner valleys tucked within the rolling slopes, from deep down in my chest,

from the dirt, I hear,

> *Do not put this energy of grief and sadness on me.*
> *That is not mine to hold. Put it down!*
> *Believe in regrowth.*
> *Share with me the energy of life.*

The energy of life?

A round-tailed ground squirrel darts out from under a clump of jojoba bushes, climbs a thorn-covered staff tearing a cholla bud off, deftly tucking it into its cheek. I inhale the bitter scent of ash picked up on the wind.

Life claims space in the midst of loss. Why does being with the energy of life in my heart feel so much harder than this reflection of death? Maybe because I do not want to do the work to truly grieve. To pick up and do small things with great love. To process the loss.

My eyes roll over the landscape searching for something familiar. This change is disorienting. I grasp for something I can recognize, for evidence like fossil impressions, a proof of the great and small which thrived just weeks before. Even the rock outcropping I know so well, positioned midway down the slope, seems jarring in its nakedness.

I don't know how to believe in the energy of life when I can't seem to register so much death. Witnessing – somehow touching opposites – requires a nimble relationship with reality. The ability to simultaneously grieve while also wholeheartedly having confidence in life.

How do I cultivate a belief in life to plant in a soil that feels dead?

Heart Remedy for Mountain Scars

Dedicated to the Catalina Mountain Range

They call you
Big

Fire

Horn

Scar

Now we share more than one-sided:
childhood want for steady
teenage neglect or need
adult designated guardian of consistency

Now we share, *something happened*
Ripped through, for you centuries grown plants and soil
for me, generations of ancestral grown skin and bone
Both precious, unique, not easy

We know how to be fierce, tie our roots to ever shifting
plate tectonics
We share beauty
cloud wisps cratered through our valleys
drops of rain that come too fast

They call me
Deformed

I could never find shoes
junior high nickname of *crippled bitch*
Anesthesia mask held unyielding over mouth by man's
hands as I begged through the plastic and gas for just
one unencumbered minute to prepare

Words fail to hold enough nuance of being split open
sideways, shuffled around, fondled from the inside
No pain scale number to describe teeth-shattering fire
which lasts for months

Numb is not absence of pain
it is the description of the void
where one sits to examine tender bits held

These pieces are so precious now
The remnants of what is left
They become new soil to work with

They call you
Horn

Fire

Scar

Big

Buffelgrass planted in our desert to feed cattle
Surgeries to coerce body to be "functional"
They always have some reason to insist poison
will fix unproductive citizen

After the allotted amount of time
my family would refuse to bring my wheelchair
Insisted pain would lessen if I just:
>   tried harder
>   did not let it stop me
>   stopped acting like a baby
>   could accept that it was time to stop using the
>   crutch

But they could never understand, crutches let one lean
brace body from ground, allow one to go further
than with these sliced-up feet

They call me
Difficult

Rebellion in refusal to hurt self for promised gain
Marked adult independence with ditched arm brace
Limbs free to curl, shutter, move with a lilt
a rhythm all my own

I know and you know that
Big

Horn

Fire

Scar

and

Fierce

Crip

Name reality
A legacy

We know better than some
      trauma sits enmeshed in survival

Our duty, believe in mending
Encode in our DNA
confidence that generations from now
they will know us
by a hundred sorted, succulent, honored names

Ritual for Sorrow

Twists like cyclone
in throat and chest,
swirls   seeks
extends tentacles to touch
something solid

      This sorrow is sacred

Becomes so much bigger
than me
when it lands
clutches desperate
breaks fingernails on rock

      This sorrow is sacred

Unsatisfied with remaining still
thrusts just below surface
creates cracks
disturbs stability
pushes into unexpected
seeks new territory
to make home and stay

      This sorrow is sacred

What to do with sacred things
which move in
eat all my stores
swarm every inch
of my greater mass
with many tiny bodies

      This sorrow is sacred

Even as it devours me

      This sorrow is sacred

So I light it for smoke and prayer
I offer sky one spark, one ember
of real
in this moment
of nothing but doubt

      This sorrow is sacred

Like all sacred things
I offer this mess
of webbed feelings
tears   unearthed fears
back to the soil

      This sorrow is sacred

It takes time
as I let go
I am full of empty

      This sorrow is sacred

I live uninhabited
barren
alone

    This sorrow is sacred

There is no going back
to the shape of before
demands new contours
bold habits to exist

    This sorrow is sacred

I pray for roots
because seed can still grow to tree
who offers ground for peace
demonstrates cycles of transformation
composts sobbing shallow breaths

    This sorrow is sacred

I
give
myself
to
hope

    This sorrow is sacred

In all sacred things
live opposites
harshness thrives alongside
gentle reminders –
inhale sweet tangy decay
soak in rain

    This sorrow is sacred

Achingly slow pace
courageous grief guides the way
      stiff joints gather tools
      toil and sweat under open sky
      devotion to repair
      reconstruct shelter
      patiently harvest time

      listen for the call
      and make contact

      This sorrow is sacred

Love as Refuge
Part 4

My city is a collection of roads, buildings, xeriscape landscapes, and carefully maintained plants from hundreds of miles away. This structure facilitates my day-to-day, encompasses my home, coffeeshops where I meet with friends, and sidewalks I wheel down. Yet, even with so much movement, my grief feels stagnant, a puddle collecting on the concrete. All I can think is, *Go to the desert.*

I ask my partner for assistance, and we find a time for him to drive me out through the cool dry air to one of the two mountain parks that sandwich the city. Finding our way down a dirt road to a parking lot full of vehicles, laughter and son jarocho music float through the air. I am annoyed, as I also try to remind myself that disability access means ease for so many people to also enjoy this place. My partner helps me slowly piece my scooter together and checks in before heading off on his own hike. I roll off down a path to find a solitary spot.

On my way, pass towering tangle of branches
Crisp tang plucked from thorny branch
Orange, plumper than pebble-sized leaves
Watermelon sweet but does not drip

Salty, like Pica sprinkled from its tiny white-and-
green plastic bag
Grind berry meat and seed with jaw, crush with teeth,
grate and crack
Desert berry bush surprise
Finger pad flesh punctured holes sting from picking,
ain't no joke
Name in English, Hackberry
Must have better names from other peoples, from
other times
I would name it Sunberry, or maybe, Bloodberry
Sweet strength

I take it as a sign that I found my spot. I wiggle out of
my scooter and onto the dirt. I hope that the voluptuous
bush blocks me enough from the tourists and that I will
not be continuously pestered about if I am okay. I briefly
think through sassy responses and how I should make
myself a sign for these times to hang on the back of
my scooter, "I am okay. Just enjoying the view." I take a
deep breath and try to stop worrying about anticipated
annoyance. I settle into what I really came here to feel.

A shadow from a passing hawk looks like it flies up
the side and over each cactus, dancing over the soil. My
sign to begin. I tell the desert my sorrow, quietly I sing
it. This verbalizing, though necessary, does not feel like
it is quite enough. I need more.

In this moment, I realize how angry I am – a big ball
ferociously swirls in my chest. Once seen, once felt,
anguish breaks through, drenching my fury. Tears drip
down my cheeks, and yet, instead of release, everything
feels trapped under a layer of despair. I lay my head
down. I surrender to the dirt.

I am finally fully present with how grief is showing
up. Body slumped. The sun is tucked behind clouds,
dulling the blazing light. Ants march, moving so fast,

it looks like they jump across the sand versus crawl. Somewhere a cardinal whistles its song.

A ritual comes because I am ready. As the chatter and laughter rises and falls in the distance, I close my eyes and imagine a bubble of pink light hovering above the ground in front of my body. My anger, worry, and despair at first drip, then stream, into this container, which stretches and expands to somehow hold it all. I say a prayer to the universe or Great Spirit for help with this part. I channel whatever I can of these emotions and thoughts into this ball until I know there is nothing more ready to leave my body. Then, I imagine this round bloated container surrounded by patient love, and send it deep into the ground. I trust that earth can compost any energy.

The next part of my ritual I do grudgingly. I ask myself for four things I can accept right now. Start with simple – the dirt is digging into my arm. I have gratitude for the hackberries that have grown this season. A fly landed and is crawling on my skin. Then more challenging – I can't control politics.

Moving off the ground back into my scooter, I feel things are not better but they do feel different. Shifted. I find there is an ounce of space to shift into.

When She Woke Me for Canyon Sunrise

The sweetness of this moment sits alongside steaming
    cups of coffee
We wait patiently in faint light
in company of cacti flower buds bloomed during night

Sunlight peeks over mountain, blesses thorns
Precious dewdrops of water
take the cue to move
are gathered by delighted lizards, beetles, dirt

A gift out of thin air no one saw coming

We sit unmoving in this canyon, where time unfolds
    slowly
face half to sun, half to shadow
shoulder to shoulder we share
soft understanding and gentle laughter
rich and nourishing
even as it evaporates

Perfect moments disappear
but paramount to loss is that they
were noticed by lizard, beetle, me

The gift is not only found in love's existence
but in the way
it slides off
drops
gives of itself
to
feed
the
roots

Interlude 5

A friend helps me put together a trough garden.
Dutifully, I plant seeds.
Birds dig them up and enjoy a delicious snack.
I have some success with the basil plant I buy from
the store and transplant into the well-watered container.
Thinking I found the answer, I buy two zucchini plants
and watch as they slowly die. Turning brown, despite
the water draining out through the container bottom.
Carrots spring tops and then stay miniature wisps of
orange.

I spray dusty clumps of nematodes to address grubs
and pests, diffusing with water to help the microbes
enter the soil to seek and infest that which is bigger
than them. Still, the ants circle the trough lip like a
highway, careful to crawl directly on the leaves, teensy
feet never touch the dirt.

Manifest reality? Bullshit.

What do you mean, set myself free? Like I do not live
in a container with only so much. We can have all we
need and still die. Abundance does not soothe what eats
us from the inside. Why should I always want more?
Wishing more into existence only means less room.

There is power in imagination. How else will we
transform this mess we are in without embracing
dreams? Somehow, I must choose self-control when

I have only known scarcity. How can I ask my heart
to relinquish the worry for food, shelter, clothes, or
medicine? Even in times with enough, I feel like I need
more stuff, security, credibility to be seen.

Change always means loss. Does not always mean
gain. Entering a shadow space where there is no horizon,
I try to swim through tumultuous emotions, keep my
head above water. But one cannot swim through dirt.
We cannot create our own seeds. We can only attend
to what has been gifted. Do I really want to pray for a
storm of change?

Do not let them smell fear. Do these pithy excretions
make anyone feel better, more powerful and controlled?
It has been a question since the beginning of time,
how does the prey survive? All nature develops coping
mechanisms, excessive reproduction, poison, thorns
– but nature has always relied on time. I wonder if
she/they/he will find a way to shake us off before our
efficient speed kills us all?

How much does my fear and anger stand in the way
of big business smothering Earth's life force? Can I be
a predator? Can I be one bird in a flock which darkens
the sky above the burning, pillaging, reaping, killing,
corporate anthills harvesting everything?

What is their purpose anyways? Did they not
manifest greed to fill the mansions? Manifest the end
to government resistance? How do we fight systems
without systems? How do we fight ourselves?

If we block out the sun, they are quick to adapt, to
turn on cleverly made lights. Or they just learn to devour
in the dark.

Over generations we have learned that there will
always be those who rally together to take what is freely
given but convince us of the need to buy more. My fear
no longer greets air, instead it balls itself up, and sinks
deeper.

To battle my own loss with what to do, to lick life's face as I also witness destructive man-made change, I dig into the trough garden's dirt, infuse hope in delicate seedlings, and try to grow something.

Neighborhood Discoveries

A wash parts the left and right side of the street
Where people walk their dogs
and planted desert trees, blessed by rainwater
swell in girth and length

Here in the low end of the city
this wash runs often with sandy water
past my neighbor's plywood door
sweeps into yard coated with little pink rocks over
    sculpted terrain

Current picks up empty vape cartridges, wrappers, bags,
    dead leaves
carries it past each grid street
amidst cracked stoop and classic car with airbrushed
    design

In this wash grows ragweed, weeping lovegrass, and
    something new
grass, but not, reedy split stock heads with brown seeds
I notice casually

Social media, friend posts a love letter to milky oats
gentle plant to work with when you need a hug
Grass, but not, thick split stock heads with brown seeds

Next trike ride, I perch in mud to pinch one seed head
it pops between my fingertips with milky exuberance
Curiosity satisfied prompts smile
Ask plant permission to use
Feel it seems happy to share
Yank out clumps, my ungraceful harvest
Triking partner waits, rolls eyes, grimaces as inquisitive
    cars drive by

I trail milky oat seeds through new avenues of my
    neighborhood
past freshly painted fences and plastic flower roadside
    shrines
Cut up straw to dry in paper bag
Slowly unwrap seed by seed to immerse in alcohol
Shake jar every day for one month
like my Nanas have done before me

Herbal remedy to sooth
Medicine from whatever is washed downstream
Made from what is offered

On This Side of the Line
Part 1

In the sky above my house
circle machines of war
My neighborhood their playground

A threat, not overseas, but a few miles from here
An invisible line drawn through desert sand

Lines drawn up in defense of a side
We are supposed to pick a side

On this line, they have built a wall
One that gets washed out every time we are blessed with
   a storm

The rivers which surge from south to north
whose flood waters overflow the arroyos they have
   carved
breach the wall
prove unpredictable power cannot be contained

But back here, in my house, in my neighborhood
Back where they pretend the border did not flip less
   than two generations ago

We learn to get good at pretending
Like my father
he pretends that he did not join his mom in the surge
    from south to north
picking cotton
filling his small-sized coffee sack compared to her bag,
    the length of a full-grown man

Now he works like he is forever proving
his worth
to be here
on this side of the line

I am the child
born so close to the land of my father's birth
A silent lineage haunts my blood
I carry stories which linger inside my body
their whispers I cannot quite hear
I feel the rhythmic echoes in my heart and skin
of migration, unhindered by all but moon, sun, water,
    wind

At the checkpoint I engage with the constant suspicion
    – do I give in or resist the questions –
Are you a citizen?
Where are you going?
What brings you here?

Fifty miles from the border and I think they wish they
    could grade from there to here
To scrape away everything which is rooted
Tear apart everything which offers hope to movement

Yet, as the line disrupts life
so does life continue to ignore the line
Butterflies migrate over
Lizards burrow underneath

Back in my home, on this land
I dig in
one side, blood sinks to meet
grafts on layers to a heart split
    links a family shattered
        assembles unbreakable roots underneath

On This Side of the Line
Part 2

In my family's borderlands
tears flood the crevices of canyons eroded by bulldozers
    and Border Patrol tires

An intergenerational devotion to duality is being torn
    away
replaced by a thirty-foot metal monument to a false
    sense of security

Plants, animals, people all try to survive without
    movement
Without movement, one can never belong
                                        Here

Contrails

Tracing trauma, one never locates the beginning
Cells encase generations of hereditary knowledge
digest compulsions to wander, act out
divides past into segments
both solid and only one slice of the story

Trauma is truth I both know and cannot quite
    understand
An itch on back of neck
Danger haunting dreams
Daily, watch one person hack away at another's
    humanity
whittle them down to that which cannot be sacrificed –
    the will to breathe

Trauma is a five-sense contact experience
Laces Italian dressing on half-eaten pasta dinner
    smacked across room
Embeds taste of hotdog mouthful with memory of being
    told, no one can ever love you the way you are
My stomach remembers echoes of screams and sobs
blockade of front door
Cower not just in body, but in heart
There is no wish fiercer than to be small enough to
    escape notice, attention, control

or big enough to drown everything unwanted out

    What to do with these people submersed in their own
        ancestral pool of unanswered atrocities
           who swim in my life
                grasping for connection?

Trauma leaves trails like snail lines crisscrossing past,
    present, future
illuminated best in a certain kind of light
I am child, adult, elder, ancestor

Elder Wisdom to Live a Good Life

Human elders, suckled on their parent's survival,
swaddled in endurance, cope. Thankfully, wind too is an
elder, as are rough rocks, thorny plants, sacred smoke,
surging flood, solid bone. They instruct: *listen to what
feels right, notice what happens with time.*

Wash in the full light of Grandmother Moon the stones I
hold for comfort, or sometimes grasp, delicately, but
with pressure, when fear and desperation rule the
moment.

Meditate, not just when I no longer remember what
ground feels like and am curled up on the inside. But
on days where I am open petal by petal toward the
sun, hollow center ready to swallow joy alive.

Make medicine. (This always takes more patience than
I imagine.) Purpose to hold attention. Focus on plants
and listen clearly. Only take what is offered and
follow guidance diligently, intuitively. When mind
wanders off, corral it back to the stove. Hold intention
for mending, as it is funneled into dark glass bottle.
After all that, remember to use it.

Do my work, even on days when I sit in confusion or shame. Writer. Who forgets words. Who can't spell. Who has no idea how to – say it right. Even on days when all I can appreciate is a bird, whose wings when spread, exhibit a thick white horizontal stripe across each wing making the muted gray surprisingly dark and richly handsome.

Seek through ritual. How and for what do I pray? I keep up on recharging the candle batteries so light burns from 9 AM to midnight, but dimming electric candles are easy to notice. How do the items on the altar reflect my now? Is there dust? I imagine myself someday with the discipline of a nun. Up, work, pray, work, pray, eat, sleep. But then I think of the nuns I have actually observed. Pray, work, sit, and devour clouds twirling across the sky... they are much better than my imagined vessels of faith at embracing grace. Practice embodying grace.

Love. This one is tricky. No matter how hard I try, loving holds the possibility of disappointment, heartbreak, loss. How do I love what is always finding purchase on the wheel of change? Relationships. My climate-change-impacted place. My unpredictable body. How do I love a glimpse of understanding before it fades? Or when I have everything to do, but the poem comes, do I let the clock fade away? Love is not held together by my arms alone but entwined with universal love, reinforced by the unstoppable rhythm of embrace, let go, embrace, let go.... Love is witnessing with clear heart.

Pause and accept the good. At 4:21 PM, the monsoon clouds, which have tauntingly gathered day after sweltering day, crack open. The opportunity is now. Remember to hit pause on DragonDictate ("Go to sleep," is the command), to gather my impatience and move outside to greet the glorious rain. The storm will be gone as fast as it came. Or the phone call from my mom, not quite at the right time, but joyous because she thought of me. Distraction is in the eye of the beholder. Bless the moments that are unscheduled.

Adaptogen Rituals

1. As we are *with* each other, we keep our promises

I bring laughter to drench brittlebush sunbeam petals
You offer durability in this moment

I let myself fall in love with your unfettered rocky soil
You listen to my heartbeat

I watch from each fallen cholla bud, life spring eternal
You send orange- and black-winged butterfly showers

As I sing tender songs of affection under a shadowed
     web of sparse shade
You stimulate with inquisitive breeze and sedate with
     afternoon warmth

2. What helps the human body adapt to states of stress?

When feeling powerless
carefully craft simple image from strokes of blue,
     fuchsia, gray
To paint is to plead, to beg, to listen

Repeat to myself, repeat to you: there is no *heal,* only
   mend
there is no going back, resolution, all better
there is only attending to now

3. Witness rituals are interventions of defiance

Each evening you invite me to assist with baking sunsets

Ingredients:
Gentle breeze
One part dust
Three parts westward sun
Generous wispy clouds

Directions:
Allow parts to combine
Provide full unwavering attention
Slowly, add bravely sung song
Mix well, until fully blended into night

Truth juices release in rest
Dash of Grandmother Moon dance
until dawn
Repeat
Makes 7.9 billion servings

4. How do I tend what feels overwhelming?

Grief is my foundation for a tenacious wild fight
For saying what needs to be said
It traces movement of jittery fear
hovers poised
coiled to strike

Grief taps me on the shoulder to know when I am being
    self-righteous
To crack severity with smile

This heartbreak side stretch can never conform to hold
    position for long
ease back toward middle
Forgive self and do what I can, where I am, with what I
    have
It may never be enough
Do it anyways

5. Faith is found in many simple actions

Practice saying thank you to
        water for washing beans clean
        wind for carrying fluted notes
        mountains for steadfast beauty
        jojoba seeds for sharing oil
        nopales for pink ruffle petaled, bee bountiful
        blooms

6. How do I orient toward space for the sacred?

My altar is covered in yucca pods and desert willow
    seeds
rocks gifted from soil
holy acorn gathered talismans
slow-growing piñon cone burst open, bountiful scent of
    change

I burn ceremonial plants to carry prayers
Adjust an assortment of metal Milagros – kidney, foot,
    lung

My altar is watched over by deities I interpret into
    existence
whom I visit between checking email and cooking
    dinner

7. Adaptogens

Are preventative and restorative
Utilize to support metabolic practices
restore intuitive balance
and digest what I cannot control

THE OFFERING

Fig. 4. "Reciprocation" © 2022 Naomi Ortiz. A uterus sheds blood which merges with oak tree roots and an

acorn, as well as, the roots of a yucca and a yucca seed pod. It gathers at the bottom in a pool to soak into the soil.

Storm Procession

Muscles tremble, I move
Wipe palms on pant legs
to better grip cane in humid desert heat

Monsoon series of storms deluge this valley
Pour themselves out, dissipate, return

Shuffle few steps on paved path
tight muscles pull on joints
Stop
ponder dirt where tiny grains of sand scatter
as scorpion shuffles away or toward
I will never know

Pain bursts from lower back
Stretch, bend
take a few steps further past ocotillo
stalks scabbed from cycle of dormancy and reanimation
thick with leaves sprouted between thorns
Onward toward bench to sit

Watershed twirled sand into silky ribbons
baked ripple under desert sun

Ephemeral river gathers what collects

carries it downstream
lowland accessible
brings the desert to me
Rocks pink, orange, flecked mica winks
torn green bark trunk trails tangle of roots
flood line marked by dried grasses plastered on
    embankment's gentle slope

My veins quiet from heart pump
breath slows
Inhale
sticky sweet creosote

In the distance
cupped by mountain desert backbone curves
clouds once lazy, stack and build
become heavy
make patchwork shadows on my arms, thighs
gradually drift over freshly carved eroded ground

Virga blooms downward thick mist
Dry air evaporates droplets before they reach desert floor
Release happens nonetheless

Embedded in acceptance
of tension, condensation, particles, pressure
a gray curtain drops
blocks distant views

Lightning kisses spark bursts of joy
Wind left out, rushes to rub cheeks
burrow face in explosions of moist sustenance

I am young to the ecology of this land
so many cacti elders, fifty to five hundred years wise
embrace when nourishment arrives
Their rosette formation of grooved leaves

channels rainwater down to the taproot
through the center

Thunder from above booms in conversation
with whispers bubbling below the surface
Dialectical wisdom
ever-dividing stalks of contradictory knowledge
rumbles
asks
What does it mean for
my body
this ecosystem
to be unapologetically disabled?

THE CLOSE

Fig. 5. "Seeking" © 2018 Naomi Ortiz. Sunset sky with pink clouds over mountain range in background. In the

middle is a cholla cactus with a flower. Thorns reflect the sun's light and roots grow down making a heart shape in the dirt.

Devotional

Ears sense song
beneath the surface
register low
melody of being alive

Bassline beat
shakes me awake
hurts my head
Bones rattle ready

Jaw clench betrays
desire for certainty
Fear throws eyes wide

Jolt of grace
accompanies
harmonic motion
l o o s e n s control

Lips part
willing to breathe
new in

Acknowledgments and Gratitudes

Several of the poems collected in this volume were previously published elsewhere, sometimes in a different version:

— "Disability Explained." 2014. https://www. naomiortiz.com/poetry-posts/poem-disability-is-the-embodiment-of-living-multiple-truths-at-once.
— "On This Side of the Line." *Poems and Numbers,* special issue "#NOF!CKINGWALL." 2018. http://poemsandnumbers.com/borderwall/ onthissideofthelinepoem/.
— "Witnessing Is Grief Work." *Instagram,* June 12, 2020. https://www.instagram.com/p/CBWaFuoBXG7/?igshi d=YmMyMTA2M2Y=
— "On This Side of the Line, Part 2." *Split This Rock,* September 2020. https://blogthisrock.blogspot. com/2020/09/poems-of-persistence-solidarity-Naomi-ortiz.html.
— "Complicating the Conversation." *Tuerspion: Magazin des Festivals Theaterformen.* 2021.
— "Found Feather Blessing." In *Held: Blessings for the Depths,* edited by M. Jade Barclay & Anna K. Blaedel Self-published, 2021.
— "Ritual for Courage" (previously titled "Heart Medicine for Courage") and "Ritual of Mutual

Attention, (previously titled, "Heart Medicine of Mutual Attention)." *About Place Journal* 6, no. 4 (October 2021). https://aboutplacejournal.org/issues/ when-we-are-lost-how-we-are-found/pollen-and-vegetation/naomi-ortiz/.

— "Benefaction." *The Texas Review* 42 (2023).

— "Nature Defined." *The Texas Review* 42 (2023).

— "Ode to Plastic Cups." In "A Forum on Disability Poetics," curated by Christopher Salerno. *Tupelo Quarterly* VI, no. 27 (2022). https://www. tupeloquarterly.com/editors-feature/a-forum-on-disability-poetics-curated-by-christopher-salerno/.

— "To Be Part of the Web of Those Who Love Place." In "Crip Ecologies: Complicate the Conversation to Reclaim Power," *POETRY Magazine,* February 1, 2022. https://www.poetryfoundation.org/poetrymagazine/ articles/157104/crip-ecologies-complicate-the-conversation-to-reclaim-power.

— "To Accept Where I Am." In *Writing the Self-Elegy: The Past Is Not Disappearing Ink,* edited by Kara Dorris. Carbondale: Southern Illinois University Press, 2023.

Note: The word "Crip" is short for "cripple" and has been reclaimed by some in the Disability community as a political expression of identity. It is an insider term to Disability community. Some Disabled folks use it, others do not. It is not appropriate for nondisabled people to use it in referring to Disabled people.

With Gratitude

The creation of this book has been supported by the best people I know.

To my partner Zach for taking this life journey with me, even when it leads down dirt roads to the middle of nowhere. For extending humor, depth, and kindness. For always being down to learn together about support and interdependence. Your love is such a gift and was a touchstone for me in writing this book.

To my writing review partners, Rachel Scoggins, Stephanie Heit, Berkley Carnine, Win-Sie Tow, and my enthusiastic volunteers, Zach Coble, Jean V., Vivian Smith, Melanie Morrison, and Lisa Hoffman who all read portions and offered encouragement and more importantly, where they got lost. Thank you for your generosity and kindness.

To Julia Watts Belser for inviting me to share in rich conversation about place.

Thanks to my writer friend Harmony Hazard for giving me permission to share her affectionately coined "mon-swoon" in Interlude 4.

To Jean and Tom V., Rachel Scoggins, Katrina Martinez, Kellie Haigh, Valerie Santos, Travonne and Vivian Smith, Dessa Cosma, Harmony Hazard, Lisette Torres-Gerald, and the core crew of the Southern Arizona Community Care Collective – Carla, Cristen, Em, Molly, Caela, and Narda, you all help me stay grounded in this amazingly dynamic place.

So much gratitude to the Turtle Disco community, hosted by Stephanie Heit and Petra Kuppers. You all are an artistic anchor, especially throughout this ongoing pandemic.

Appreciation to the incredibly talented individuals who make up Zoeglossia for working toward amplifying Disability poetics. Special thanks to Jennifer Bartlett, Sheila Black, Connie Voisine, and other staff who support Zoeglossia, and who sent out an email asking, "Who has a manuscript?" And to Rigoberto Gonzalez for saying I had something here.

To the Ancestors who travel with me and hold my hand in the darkness, to my ever mysterious and present relationship with Great Spirit, as well as to my mentor, the beautiful Sonoran Desert, I continue to be awed and inspired by your depths.

A special thank-you to Erin Manning, Vincent W.J. van Gerven Oei, and everyone at 3Ecologies and punctum books. Thank you for believing in this book, making it beautiful, and investing in open-source options to support accessibility.

Many thanks to all the readers, librarians, and bookstore folks who labor to connect books with the world.

Lastly, to Marlin Thomas, still following your advice to put it all on the page.

Bibliography

Burnett, John. "Border Wall Rising in Arizona, Raises Concerns among Conservationists, Native Tribes." *NPR*, October 13, 2019. https://www.npr.org/2019/10/13/769444262/border-wall-rising-in-arizona-raises-concerns-among-conservationists-native-trib.

Chandler, Claire. "Arizona's Mount Graham Red Squirrel Makes Comeback, But Not Out of the Woods Yet." *Tucson.com,* November 17, 2020. https://tucson.com/news/local/arizonas-mount-graham-red-squirrel-makes-comeback-but-not-out-of-the-woods-yet/article_f4fda664-723b-58db-bfa7-7b483a82636c.html.

Gardner, Jeff. "How Dry We Are: Monsoon 2020 Second Worst in the Record Books." *Tucson Weekly,* October 1, 2020. https://www.tucsonweekly.com/TheRange/archives/2020/10/01/how-dry-we-are-monsoon-2020-second-worst-in-the-record-books.

NDTV. "'How Dare You?': 16-Year-Old Greta Thunberg Thunders at UN Climate Summit." *YouTube,* September 24, 2019. https://www.youtube.com/watch?v=M103NCPKZ4U.

Kiser, Matt. *What the Fuck Just Happened Today?* https://whatthefuckjusthappenedtoday.com/.

Lindsey, Rebecca. "Climate Change: Atmospheric Carbon Dioxide." *NOAA Climate.gov,* June 23, 2022. https://

www.climate.gov/news-features/understanding-climate/climate-change-atmospheric-carbon-dioxide.

Ortiz, Naomi. *Sustaining Spirit: Self-Care for Social Justice.* Berkley: Reclamation Press, 2018.

"PFAS Explained." *Environmental Protection Agency,* April 10, 2023. https://www.epa.gov/pfas/pfas-explained.

"Quitobaquito Springs." *National Park Service,* June 24, 2018. https://www.nps.gov/orpi/learn/historyculture/quitobaquito-springs.htm.

Reznick, Alisa. "Standoff with Border Patrol, National Park Service Ends in Scuffle with Indigenous-Led Demonstrators." *Arizona Public Media,* September 22, 2020. https://news.azpm.org/p/news-splash/2020/9/22/180618-stand-off-with-border-patrol-national-park-service-ends-in-scuffle-with-indigenous-led-demonstrators/.

"Saguaro Cactus." *National Park Service,* January 6, 2016. https://www.nps.gov/orpi/learn/nature/saguaro-cactus.htm.